Accounting Without Anxiety

Making Numbers Work for Your Business
(and Your Peace of Mind)

Antonio Pascarella

Clarity Works Publishing - Meriden, Connecticut

Accounting Without Anxiety
Making Numbers Work for Your Business — and for Your Peace of Mind

Published by Clarity Works Publishing
An imprint of StoneGate Publishing Group, LLC
48 S Broad Ter, Meriden, CT 06450
www.stonegatepublishinggroup.com
Permissions & inquiries: permissions@stonegatepublishinggroup.com
Bulk orders & speaking: partnerships@stonegatepublishinggroup.com

ISBNs:
Hardcover: 979-8-9999855-0-7
Paperback: 979-8-9999855-1-4
eBook (EPUB/Kindle): 979-8-9999855-2-1

Library of Congress Control Number: 2025946556

First edition, September 2025
Printed in the United States of America

Printer's key: 10 9 8 7 6 5 4 3 2 1

Disclaimer

This publication is for educational and informational purposes only and does not constitute accounting, tax, financial, legal, or other professional advice. Every business situation is unique; readers should consult qualified professionals before making decisions. The author and publisher make no representations or warranties regarding the accuracy or completeness of the contents and expressly disclaim liability for any loss or damage arising from the use of this material. Examples are illustrative; results may vary.

Trademarks
All trademarks, service marks, product names, and logos appearing in this book are the property of their respective owners. Their use does not imply affiliation with or endorsement by them.

Credits
Editing: Antonio Pascarella
Interior design & typesetting: StoneGate Publishing, LLC
Cover design: StoneGate Publishing, LLC
Cover illustration/icons: Antonio Pascarella
Text set in Garamond 11/15 on 6"×9" trim.

Manufacturing & Distribution
Manufactured in the United States of America.

Contact
StoneGate Publishing, LLC•
48 S Broad Ter, Meriden, CT 06450
www.stonegatepublishinggroup.com
info@stonegatepublishinggroup.com

To every small business owner who has ever stayed up late worrying about payroll, invoices, or taxes — this book is for you. May it bring you clarity, confidence, and peace of mind.

And also, to all our current clients, whose trust and partnership inspire us daily to make accounting a tool for growth, not stress.

Table of Contents

Preface

I didn't set out to write a book about accounting.

In fact, if you had told me years ago that I'd be spending my time teaching business owners how to manage their numbers, I might have laughed. But after working with hundreds of entrepreneurs, one truth kept surfacing: most small businesses don't fail because of a lack of passion or talent. They fail because of money mismanagement.

Not because owners don't care. Not because they're lazy. But because no one ever explained accounting in a way that made sense. Too often, it's buried in jargon, spreadsheets, or conversations with accountants that feel more like lectures than guidance.

I wanted to change that.

What I've seen working with hundreds of small businesses is this: many owners look at their accountant as just another monthly invoice. If you treat accountancy as an expense, that's exactly what you'll get — an expense. But when you treat your accountant as a strategic partner, you unlock insights that can grow and even transform your business.

Too often, business owners will pay a coach twenty times more than their accountant, even though the accountant has access to the financial truths that drive real growth. I've seen bad advice from self-proclaimed coaches sink businesses, while sound advice from accountants goes ignored simply because it's seen as "extra cost." The result? Lost opportunities, slower growth, and sometimes the painful closing of doors.

The advice I want to leave with you is simple: change your mindset. Stop seeing your accountant as an expense. See them as a partner in your success. Because at the end of the day, your success is our success.

This book is for every business owner who has ever looked at a financial report and felt like it was written in a foreign language, waited until tax season to find out if they were profitable, avoided opening a bill or statement out of fear, or wondered, "Am I even doing this right?"

If that sounds like you, this book is your companion. It's not here to impress accountants. It's here to empower you.

I've seen too many brilliant businesses close their doors because the numbers weren't managed. And I've seen ordinary businesses thrive simply because the owner developed the right financial habits. My hope is that this book helps you join the second group.

Read it with a pen in hand. Dog-ear the pages. Apply the lessons one at a time. And most importantly, remember this: you don't have to be an accountant to run a financially strong business. You just need the right tools and a willingness to use them.

This book is my way of putting those tools in your hands.

— Antonio Pascarella

Chapter 1 — Why Every Business Owner Must Understand Accounting

The Silent Killer of Small Businesses

Most small businesses don't close because their product is bad, their idea is flawed, or because the owner isn't willing to work hard enough.

They close for a reason that feels far less dramatic — yet far more dangerous.

The money simply… runs out for a variety of reasons.

Sometimes it's a slow, almost invisible leak. Expenses inch upward — rent creeps higher, supplier prices rise, payroll grows, sales price increases delayed — until profit margins quietly dissolve. It doesn't happen overnight; it happens in small, almost imperceptible steps, the kind that are easy to dismiss as "just part of doing business."

As most likely all accountants have experienced and tried to correct, small business owners' tapping into the business resources or treating the business as their own personal wallet is also another major issue. The business needs to be nurtured from inception to self-sustainment.

Other times, it's a single, devastating blow. A surprise tax bill. A piece of critical equipment breaking down. A major customer who suddenly decides not to pay. One moment, the business seems healthy. The next, it's gasping for air.

What's truly frustrating is that, in many cases, the warning signs existed months — sometimes years — before the collapse. They were right there, buried in the numbers.

But the owner never saw them.

Not because they were careless. Not because they didn't care. But because they were running their business without the one thing that could have shown them the truth — a clear, accurate picture of their finances. They were flying blind.

And this is where accounting stops being "paperwork" and starts being survival. Every business needs accounting (and an accountant to go over the numbers' story) and any business owner believing that he or she is able to wear the already-so-many-hats, will eventually realize that something must be given up and get the help needed to read the business' stories, present and future, from the numbers.

Good accounting doesn't just record the past — it reveals the future. It shows you trends before they become problems. It turns hidden risks into visible decisions. And it gives you the power to fix what's broken before it's too late.

In short, accounting can mean the difference between a business that quietly fades away… and one that thrives for decades.

Accounting Is Not Just for Accountants

For many business owners, "accounting" is something that happens somewhere else — a back-office task delegated to a bookkeeper or CPA. It's a chore. A necessary evil. A pile of receipts that gets dumped on someone's desk at tax time with the hope that everything will come out right.

That approach might be enough if your only ambition is to avoid a letter from the IRS. But if your real goal is to grow your business, stay profitable, and make confident, well-informed decisions, you can't treat accounting as something you hand off and forget.

You can outsource bookkeeping. You can hire a CPA to prepare your taxes. But you cannot outsource *financial awareness*.

Why? Because in the end, you're the one making the calls.
You make the calls.
An accountant can tell you your gross margin has dropped 5%, or advise you on what you should or not be doing, he or she will tell you why you should or not be doing what you are doing, but they can't decide whether you should raise prices, renegotiate vendor contracts, or eliminate low-margin products. Those are strategic moves that only you — with your knowledge of the market, customers, and operations — can make. If you don't understand the numbers, you're making those decisions in the dark.

You catch problems earlier.
If you look at your own financial reports every week or two, you won't be blindsided. You'll notice if sales slow down in a particular product line, if expenses creep up in a certain department, or if cash flow is tightening. These small warning signs give you time to adjust — while the problem is still manageable. Waiting to look at a quarterly report could mean discovering the issue three months too late.

You speak the language of money.

Whether you're talking to a lender, an investor, or even a supplier you're negotiating terms with, credibility matters. When you can clearly explain your margins, cash flow position, and growth trends without constantly saying, "I'll have to check with my accountant," you project confidence and competence. You become someone they trust with their money — because you clearly understand your own.

The truth is, accounting isn't just about recording what's happened — it's about giving you the power to influence what happens next.

And the more you, as the owner, stay connected to your numbers, the more control you'll have over your business's future.

Case Study: Two Owners, Two Outcomes

Both Sarah and Mike owned small but growing coffee shops in different parts of town. Each had a loyal customer base, a decent product, and a steady stream of sales.

Sarah's approach: She met with her tax accountant once a year at tax time. Beyond that, she barely glanced at her numbers. Her focus was on making customers happy and creating a great atmosphere — important things, but she assumed the "money side" was handled by her bookkeeper.

When her coffee bean supplier quietly raised prices three times in 12 months, Sarah didn't notice. She also didn't realize her labor costs had crept up as she added part-time staff to cover "just in case" shifts.

By the time she looked at her year-end profit and loss statement, her net profit had dropped from 15% to barely breaking even. She tried raising prices to recover, but customers resisted, and it was too late to make gradual adjustments.

Mike's approach: Mike also had a bookkeeper and an accountant, but he looked at his profit-and-loss report every two weeks. He tracked his average cost per cup, labor as a percentage of sales, and monthly cash flow.

When his supplier raised prices, Mike saw the impact immediately. Instead of absorbing the increase, he tested a small price adjustment and negotiated a better rate with a different vendor. When labor costs ticked up, he tweaked scheduling to better match peak hours.

At year's end, Mike's profit margin actually *increased* — despite the same supplier price hikes and market conditions that hit Sarah's business.
The difference wasn't luck. It was engagement. Mike didn't do his own books, but he *understood* his numbers and used them to steer his business. Sarah outsourced not just the work, but the awareness — and paid the price.

What the case study tells is that if a business owner sees the outsourcing of the bookkeeping and awareness but sees these resource as an expense, he or she doesn't understand the importance of accounting. Accounting is an added-value to the business, not as an expense.

The Three Roles of Accounting in a Small Business

Think of accounting not as a single task, but as a three-part system that works together to keep your business alive and moving in the right direction.

1. Recordkeeping — *The History Log*

   Every sale, every expense, every payroll run, every tax payment — it all gets logged.

   It's not glamorous. Nobody frames their receipts or throws a party when the books balance at month-end. But accurate recordkeeping is the bedrock of your business's financial health.

   If the records are sloppy or incomplete, every other part of accounting becomes useless. Your financial statements are not accurate; thus, you might make the wrong decisions and steer your business where it is not desired; at tax time, you would provide those very same financial statements to your tax accountants and you might be overpaying (or underpaying) your tax obligations. It all starts with the recordkeeping. Do it incorrectly, everything else will reflect an incorrect picture of your business. You can't trust reports that are built on bad data, and you can't make good decisions if the facts aren't right in the first place.

   Example: Imagine a pilot trying to fly a plane with an altimeter that sometimes lies. It doesn't matter how skilled the pilot is — they're in danger. Your books are that instrument panel. They have to be correct, every time.

2. Reporting — *The Scoreboard*
   Raw data is just a pile of numbers. Reporting turns that pile into something readable and meaningful.
   Your Profit & Loss statement shows whether the business is actually making money. Your balance sheet shows what you own and what you owe. Your cash flow statement reveals how money is moving in and out. These reports are your scoreboard — they tell you if you're winning, losing, or just treading water. They highlight patterns, such as seasonal dips in sales or rising costs in a certain category, so you can see the bigger picture instead of just guessing.

   Example: A basketball coach doesn't make game decisions based on how the crowd is cheering — they look at the scoreboard. In business, reports are that scoreboard.

3. Decision-Making — *The Steering Wheel*
   This is where most small businesses stumble. They have records. They have reports. But they never take the next step: using them.
   The real power of accounting comes when you look at the numbers and act on them. When you see profit margins shrinking and decide whether to raise prices, cut costs, or focus on higher-margin products. When you notice a cash crunch coming and decide whether to speed up collections or delay a purchase.

   Without this step, your records and reports are just expensive paperwork. With it, they become a steering

wheel that lets you guide the business toward your goals
— and away from danger.

Example: Driving with your hands in your lap while the
car's steering wheel spins freely isn't "letting the car do its
thing." It's a crash waiting to happen. Your numbers tell
you when to turn. You still have to take the wheel.

When all three roles work together — accurate recordkeeping,
clear reporting, and decisive action — accounting stops being
"something you have to do" and becomes one of your most
valuable business tools.

The Three Roles of Accounting in a Small Business

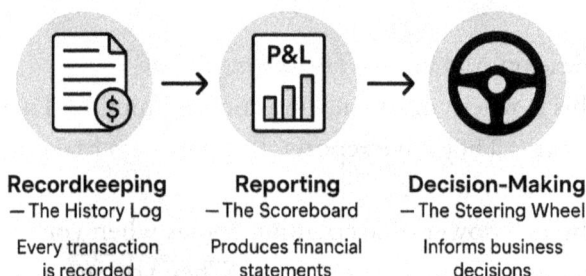

Recordkeeping	Reporting	Decision-Making
— The History Log	— The Scoreboard	— The Steering Wheel
Every transaction is recorded	Produces financial statements	Informs business decisions

Figure 1: The Three Roles of Accounting

Driving Without a Dashboard

Picture this: you're cruising down the highway in a car with no
fuel gauge, no speedometer, and no warning lights. The engine
sounds fine. The ride feels smooth. Everything *seems* okay —
right up until the moment the car sputters, stalls, and

leaves you stranded on the shoulder. Or worse, the engine overheats and blows because you had no clue it was in trouble. Running a business without paying attention to your accounting reports is exactly the same.

Your reports are your dashboard. Without them, you're not really driving — you're coasting, blindfolded, and hoping for the best.

- Fuel Gauge: Cash Flow Report
  This tells you how much usable cash you have and how long it will last at your current burn rate. Without it, you might think you're fine because you have cash in the bank account, "sales are good," not realizing you are days away from running dry.
- Speedometer: Sales Trends
  Are you accelerating or losing momentum? Weekly and monthly sales reports show if your growth is picking up speed or if you're slowing down — so you can act before you come to a standstill.
- Warning Lights: Expense Reports, Overdue Invoices, Debt Levels
  These are the early alerts that trouble is coming. A sudden spike in expenses, a growing list of customers who haven't paid, or rising debt balances are all flashing lights that tell you to pull over and address the problem before it becomes an emergency.
-

The truth is, coasting with your eyes closed feels fine — right up until the crash. Checking your business dashboard regularly doesn't just prevent disasters; it gives you the

confidence to drive faster, take calculated turns, and actually
enjoy the ride, knowing you're in control.

Figure 2: The Business Dashboard Analogy

Case Study: Two Coffee Shops, Two Outcomes

Let's compare two scenarios:

Case 1 — "Coffee & Latte Bar"

Jewel checks her cash flow every Monday morning.

In April, she notices her wholesale coffee bean costs have risen
12% over the past two months.

She quickly negotiates with her supplier, adjusts menu prices
slightly, and updates her inventory process.

Result: profits stay consistent, and customers barely notice the
price change.

Case 2 — "Crew & Brew"

The owner hands all receipts to a bookkeeper once a quarter.

By the time he gets the quarterly report, the higher coffee bean
costs have been eating into profits for months.

By then, raising prices feels risky because cash reserves are low.

Result: He takes on a small loan to cover operating costs, increasing debt and stress.

The only difference between Jewel and the other owner? **Jewel treated accounting like a daily business tool, not a once-a-year obligation.**

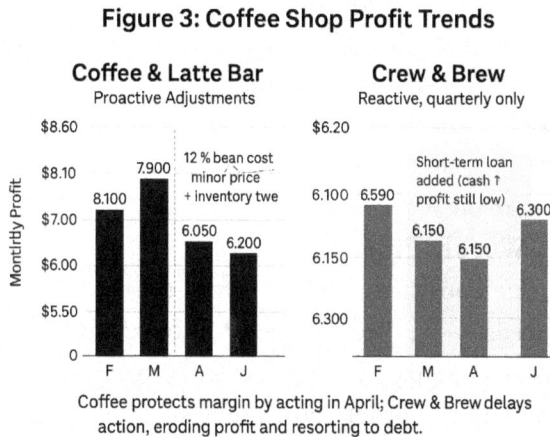

Figure 3: Coffee Shop Profit Trends

Coffee & Latte Bar
Proactive Adjustments

Crew & Brew
Reactive, quarterly only

Coffee protects margin by acting in April; Crew & Brew delays action, eroding profit and resorting to debt.

Figure 3: Coffee Shop Profit Trends

Accounting = Clarity

When you understand your numbers, you:

- Know your break-even point (the minimum sales you need to cover costs).
- Can forecast slow seasons and plan for them.
- Recognize which products or services are most profitable.
- Avoid unnecessary debt by managing cash proactively.
- Sleep better because you're not guessing.

How to Make Accounting a Habit

Most business owners don't fail because they *never* look at their
numbers — they fail because they don't look at them *often enough*
or they don't use the tools available to help them read their
business' story. Your accountant provides the tools you need to
understand your business' story but if you are only seeing the
service as a monthly expense, you are missing out on the most
important tool you and your business possess. Accounting only
works as a business tool if it's a regular part of your routine, not
an occasional fire drill.

Here's how to make it second nature:

1. **Set a Weekly Finance Day**
   Pick one consistent day each week to review your
   financials — and treat it like an unbreakable appointment.
   Monday mornings can set the tone for the week, while
   Friday afternoons let you wrap things up before the
   weekend.
   On this day, look at:
   - Total sales for the week
   - Any unusual expenses
   - Current cash balance
   - Overdue invoices or late customer payments
2. Bills you owe in the next 7 days
   This quick check-in takes 15–30 minutes but can save you
   from nasty surprises.
3. **Use Software That Speaks Plain English**
   Accounting software should *simplify*, not intimidate. Tools
   like QuickBooks, Xero, and Wave offer visual dashboards
   that turn complex data into clear charts

4. and graphs.

    Instead of staring at a wall of numbers, you can see:

    - Sales trends over time
    - Expense categories in pie charts
    - Cash flow movement in and out of your business

    The easier the software is to read, the more likely you are to use it regularly.

5. **Ask "Why?" — Every Time**

    Numbers are signals, not the full story. If sales drop, ask "Why?" until you find the root cause. Was it seasonality? A marketing campaign that ended? A competitor's new promotion?

    If expenses spike, ask "Why?" until you know whether it's a one-time cost or a permanent change.

    Treat your financials like a doctor treats symptoms: the goal isn't just to *see* them, but to diagnose what's really happening.

6. **Get Comfortable With Your Reports**

    You don't have to prepare your own Profit & Loss, Balance Sheet, or Cash Flow Statement — but you *do* need to read them. Every month, without fail.

    - Profit & Loss (P&L) tells you whether you made money or lost it.
    - Balance Sheet shows what you own and what you owe.
    - Cash Flow Statement explains how cash actually moved in and out, which is often different from "profit."

    The more familiar these reports become, the

- faster you'll spot trends — and the more confident you'll feel making decisions.

How to Make Accounting a Habit

Set a Weekly
Finance Day

Use Software
That Speaks Plain
English

Ask „Why?"—
Every Time

Get Comfortable
With Your Reports

Figure 4: The Accounting Habit Loop

Action Steps for This Week

- Schedule a 30-minute "money meeting" with yourself and your team (or your accountant) every week. If you don't already have accounting software, research and choose one by the end of the month. If you are unsure as to which software gives you all the tools you need, ask your accountant.
- Ask your bookkeeper or accountant to explain your latest Profit & Loss statement in plain language. Again, do not think of their services as an expense. They are value-added to your business and are giving you the tools you need to succeed.
- Write down three financial questions you want answered about your business — and commit to finding those answers before next week.

Chapter Recap

You don't have to become a CPA to run your business — but you **do** have to understand your own numbers.

Accounting is your GPS, your dashboard, your warning system, and your scoreboard.

Without it, you're driving blind. With it, you're in control.

In the next chapter, we'll break down the **three essential financial statements** — Balance Sheet, Profit & Loss, and Cash Flow — and show you exactly how to read them.

Chapter 2 — The Core Financial Statements

Why Financial Statements Matter

Imagine you're about to invest in a business — maybe even your own.
Would you risk your hard-earned money based solely on gut instinct?
Would you trust a handshake and a smile without knowing the facts?
Of course not.
You'd want to see proof — numbers that tell the real story.

Financial statements are that proof. They are the official record of your business's financial health — an x-ray that reveals what's really going on behind the scenes.

Too many small business owners assume these reports are only for banks, investors, or the IRS.
But here's the truth: **they are first and foremost for you**.

If you don't use them, you're like a pilot refusing to check the instrument panel mid-flight.

What They Tell You

At their core, financial statements give you answers to the three most important business questions:

1. Are we making money?
   Your Profit & Loss Statement (P&L) shows if your sales are covering your costs and generating profit — not just this month, but over time.

2. A positive "gut feeling" can mask the reality that your margins are shrinking.

3. How much cash do we really have — and how fast is it moving?
   Your Cash Flow Statement tracks money in and out, showing whether you have enough to pay tomorrow's bills, not just whether you were "profitable" last quarter. Many businesses fail while profitable on paper simply because they ran out of cash.

4. What do we own vs. what do we owe?
   The Balance Sheet reveals your assets and your debts. This tells you your true net worth — the actual value of your business if you sold everything today and paid off what you owe.

Why This Matters More Than You Think

Without financial statements, every decision you make — from hiring a new employee to buying new equipment — is based on guesswork. And in business, guessing is expensive.

Think about it:
- Hiring without numbers might mean adding payroll you can't afford in three months.
- Expanding without numbers might mean taking on debt when your cash reserves can't handle the payments.
- Pricing without numbers might mean selling your best product at a loss without realizing it.

Figure 1: Gut Feeling vs. Data-Driven Decisions
Split-panel graphic showing:
Left side: A business owner looking confident but surrounded by question marks ("Guessing").
Right side: Same owner reviewing charts and graphs ("Informed Decisions").

The Real-World Cost of Ignoring Your Financials

In 2023, a regional catering company expanded aggressively into new venues.

They *thought* their margins were healthy because sales were up 40%.

When they finally reviewed their P&L in detail, they realized their cost of goods had spiked, wiping out nearly all their profit.

By the time they caught it, the expansion had drained their cash, forcing them to take a high-interest loan just to keep operating.

This wasn't a bad product, bad team, or bad market — it was a bad decision made in the dark.

Bottom Line

Financial statements aren't "nice to have." They are the lifeline of your business.

They give you:

- Clarity — You know exactly where you stand.
- Control — You make proactive, not reactive, decisions.
- Confidence — You can speak to lenders, investors, or even your staff with authority.

Without them, you're steering blind — and no amount of hard work can make up for not knowing where you're going.

The Three Essential Financial Statements

Every small business, no matter the industry, should understand these three:

1. Profit & Loss Statement (P&L) — *Also called the Income Statement*

   - The P&L tells the story of your business's performance over a period of time — usually monthly, quarterly, or annually.
   - It answers the simplest yet most important question: "Did we make money?"

   A typical P&L includes:

   - Revenue (Sales) — All income from products or services sold.
   - Cost of Goods Sold (COGS) — Direct costs of producing your goods/services.
   - Gross Profit — Revenue minus COGS — a measure of efficiency in production.

- Operating Expenses — Rent, salaries, marketing, utilities, insurance, and other overhead.
- Net Profit (or Loss) — What's left after *everything*, including taxes.

Why it matters:

Helps you evaluate if your pricing, sales volume, and cost control are working together.

Shows profitability trends over time.

Enables quick identification of problem areas (e.g., a sudden rise in COGS or marketing spending).

Example:

A catering business may have record-high sales in December, but if they also faced a huge spike in ingredient costs and seasonal staffing, the P&L might reveal a slimmer-than-expected profit margin.

2. Balance Sheet — *A snapshot of what your business owns and owes*

The Balance Sheet is a moment-in-time report showing your business's assets, liabilities, and equity.

It follows the equation:

- Assets = Liabilities + Equity

Sections include:

- Assets — Cash, accounts receivable, inventory, property, equipment.
- Liabilities — Short-term obligations (accounts payable, credit cards) and long-term debts (loans, mortgages).

- Equity — The owner's stake in the business after debts are subtracted from assets.

Why it matters:
It tells you if you can cover your short-term obligations (liquidity).
Shows whether your business is building net worth or sinking into debt.
Reveals the capital structure — how much is funded by owners vs. creditors.

Example:
A retail store may show $150,000 in assets, but if $140,000 of that is financed through loans and credit, the owner has only $10,000 in equity — a sign of high leverage.

3. Cash Flow Statement — *Tracks the movement of cash in and out of your business*

The Cash Flow Statement bridges the gap between profit and actual liquidity.
It's divided into three sections:

- Operating Activities — Cash from regular business operations (customer payments, supplier payments, wages).
- Investing Activities — Cash used for or received from buying/selling assets, property, or equipment.
- Financing Activities — Loans, repayments, owner's draws, issuing shares.

Why it matters:
A business can be profitable on paper but broke in reality if customers are slow to pay.
Shows timing issues that could lead to a cash crunch.
Helps plan for major purchases or expansion without risking insolvency.

Example:
A manufacturing company might report a $30,000 quarterly profit but negative $20,000 cash flow because customers haven't paid large invoices yet. This means the business needs a short-term funding solution to cover payroll and rent.

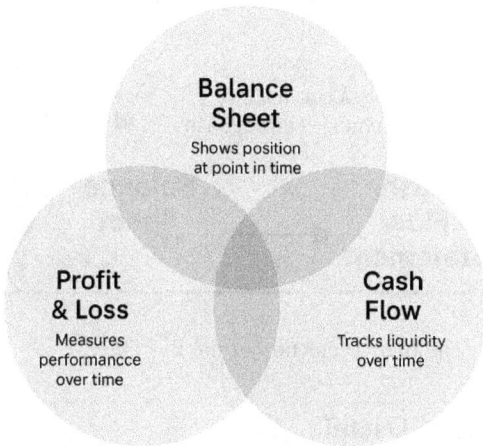

Balance Sheet
Shows position
at point in time

Profit & Loss
Measures
performancce
over time

Cash Flow
Tracks liquidity
over time

Figure 2: The Three Statements at a Glance

How They Work Together
These three statements aren't isolated reports — they are interlinked.

- **The P&L** feeds into the **Balance Sheet** by updating retained earnings or owner's/member's equity (part of equity).
- **The Balance Sheet** connects to the **Cash Flow Statement** through changes in assets and liabilities.
- **The Cash Flow Statement** explains the actual liquidity position, which affects your ability to operate even if the P&L looks good.

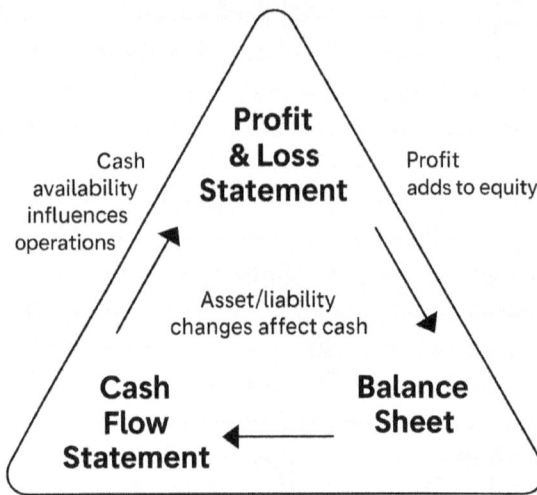

Figure 3: The Interconnection of the Big Three

Making These Reports Useful
1. **Review Monthly** — Don't wait until tax season.
2. **Compare Periods** — Month-to-month and year-to-year comparisons reveal trends.
3. **Ask Questions** — Don't just look at numbers; ask why they changed.
4. **Use Visuals** — Charts can reveal patterns hidden in raw data.

Action Steps for This Week
- Pull your last three months of P&L, Balance Sheet, and Cash Flow reports.
- Circle at least three numbers you don't understand and research or ask your accountant about them.
- Compare this month's numbers to the same month last year — note any trends.
- Create a simple dashboard that shows:
  o Monthly sales
  o Monthly expenses
  o Cash on hand

Chapter Recap

Financial statements aren't just paperwork — they're decision-making tools.

Once you learn to read them, you'll be able to:
- Spot trouble early.
- Plan for growth.
- Communicate confidently with lenders, investors, and partners.

In the next chapter, we'll take this a step further and look at **Cash Flow Mastery** later — how to predict, protect, and grow your cash so you're never caught short.

Chapter 3 – Setting Up Your Accounting System

Choosing the Right Software

When you launch a business, your first instinct might be to keep things lean. Many entrepreneurs start by tracking income and expenses in Excel or Google Sheets. It feels simple, flexible, and cheap. But what works with 20 transactions a month becomes unmanageable when you're handling hundreds.

As your business grows, spreadsheets become a liability:

- Errors multiply. A missed formula or wrong cell reference can throw off your totals.
- No audit trail. It's hard to know *who changed what and when.*
- Limited reporting. Building a proper cash flow statement in Excel requires accounting skills most business owners don't have time for.
- Tax headaches. When tax season rolls around, you or your accountant have to sort through raw data rather than clean reports.

This is where accounting software shines. It's not just about recordkeeping; it's about giving you real-time insights, efficiency, and peace of mind.

Popular Options

There are dozens of systems on the market, but four names dominate for small businesses:

1. **QuickBooks Online (QBO)**
    o   Strengths: The market leader in the U.S., widely recognized by accountants and tax preparers. It offers robust reporting, payroll options, and an enormous marketplace of integrations (apps for inventory, CRM, ecommerce, etc.).
    o   Consider if: You need a system that scales as you grow, and you want confidence that any accountant you hire will know the platform.
    o   Watch out for: The interface can feel intimidating to non-accountants, and the monthly fees increase with more advanced features.

2. **Xero**
    o   Strengths: Known for its user-friendly design and unlimited users (no extra cost per seat, unlike QuickBooks). Excellent for businesses that operate internationally, since multi-currency handling is built in.
    o   Consider if: You want a clean, modern experience with strong integrations, especially if you collaborate with multiple partners, bookkeepers, or advisors.
    o   Watch out for: Some advanced features (like job costing) require third-party add-ons.

3. **Wave**
    o   Strengths: Free core accounting features. Perfect for freelancers and solopreneurs who need the basics: invoicing, expense tracking, and simple reporting.

o Consider if: You're just starting out, have minimal transaction volume, and want to avoid upfront costs (however, consider the business growth and ease of data portability to other platforms).

o Watch out for: Limited support, weaker reporting, and fewer integrations. You may outgrow it quickly.

4. **FreshBooks**

o Strengths: Tailored to service-based businesses. Excellent invoicing, time tracking, and expense categorization. Very intuitive for non-accountants.

o Consider if: You're a consultant, freelancer, or agency that bills by the hour or project.

o Watch out for: Weaker on inventory management and less robust financial reporting.

Key Features to Look For

Every business has unique needs, but here are the "must-haves" that will make your life easier:

- **Bank Feeds**: Directly connects your bank accounts and credit cards to pull in transactions daily. No more manual entries.
    - o *Example:* Instead of typing in every Starbucks coffee, the expense flows in automatically and you just tag it as "Meals & Entertainment."
- **Invoicing**: Look for systems that allow you to:
    - o Customize invoices with your branding.
    - o Accept credit card or ACH payments directly through the invoice.

- o Track unpaid invoices and send automatic reminders.
- o *Example:* A photographer can send a client invoice with a "Pay Now" button — reducing collection time from weeks to days.
- **Expense Tracking & Receipt Capture**: Snap a picture of a receipt with your phone and let the software categorize it. This not only saves time but keeps you audit-ready.
- **Reporting**: At minimum, you should be able to run:
  - o Profit & Loss (Income Statement)
  - o Balance Sheet
  - o Cash Flow Statement
    Advanced platforms also offer dashboards with KPIs like gross margin, receivables aging, and expense breakdowns.
- **Payroll Integration**: If you pay employees or contractors, seamless payroll saves hours. Taxes, withholdings, and benefits flow straight into your books without double entry. Make sure you have complete administrative access to all the payroll modules. You don't want to "change the bank
- account in your accounting software" and later find out that you had to call the vendor to make that change; or if there is a mistake on a payroll, you need the appropriate level of control to prevent any data to live on your balance sheet indefinitely.
- **Mobile App**: Essential for business owners on the go. Capture receipts, check balances, and approve invoices from your phone.

How to Choose Based on Business Size & Complexity

- **Freelancers / Solopreneurs**
  - o Best fit: Wave (free) or FreshBooks (for client billing).
  - o Priorities: Simple invoicing, basic expense tracking, easy tax reporting.
- **Small Teams (1–10 employees)**
  - o Best fit: QuickBooks Online or Xero.
  - o Priorities: Robust reporting, payroll, scalability, and integrations (CRM, inventory, ecommerce).
- **Product-Based Businesses with Inventory**
  - o Best fit: QuickBooks Online with inventory add-ons, or Xero with inventory apps like DEAR Systems.
  - o Priorities: Real-time tracking of stock levels, cost of goods sold, and purchase orders.
- **Service-Based Agencies or Firms**
  - o Best fit: FreshBooks or Xero (with time tracking add-ons).
  - o Priorities: Project profitability, billable hours, client retainer management.
- **Global Businesses / Multi-Currency Needs**
  - o Best fit: Xero.
  - o Priorities: Automatic exchange rate adjustments, multi-currency invoicing, and foreign bank account feeds.

Pro Tip #1: Don't just think about what works today. Ask: *"What will I need if my revenue doubles in two years?"* The cost and disruption of switching systems later is far higher than choosing one that's a little more powerful than you need right now.

Pro Tip #2: Don't think your accounting software "does the job for you". It does not. You still need to proactively post your transactions in whichever income/expense/liability/equity they belong. It does not replace your bookkeeper, accountant, or tax accountant.

Cloud-Based vs Desktop Systems

Cloud-Based Systems (QuickBooks Online, Xero, Wave, FreshBooks)
- Accessible from anywhere with internet.
- Automatic updates and backups.
- Connect easily with banks and apps.
- Subscription model (monthly fees).

Example: An accountant traveling between client sites can pull up real-time financials on their phone or tablet.

Desktop Systems (QuickBooks Desktop, Sage 50)
- Installed locally on one or more computers.
- Often cheaper over the long run if you don't need integrations.
- Doesn't require internet, which can be useful in areas with poor connectivity.
- Requires manual backups and updates.

Example: A small manufacturing company in a rural area may prefer desktop QuickBooks if cloud reliability is questionable.

The trend is clear: for most modern small businesses, the cloud environment is the smart choice. It reduces IT headaches, allows collaboration (your accountant can log in anytime), and provides real-time data. Desktop may still fit if your industry has unique software needs or you require offline access.

Putting It All Together

Choosing accounting software isn't about bells and whistles; it's about freeing your time and clarifying your numbers. The right system ensures:

- You spend less time on admin and more on running your business.
- You always know where you stand financially.
- You avoid costly surprises at tax season or when applying for loans.

Think of software not as an expense, but as an investment in decision-making clarity. The sooner you move off spreadsheets and into a professional system, the faster you can grow with confidence.

Chapter 4 – Bookkeeping Fundamentals

Accounting vs Bookkeeping

Many entrepreneurs confuse "accounting" with "bookkeeping." They're related but not identical. Think of bookkeeping as the daily upkeep of your financial garden: watering, pruning, and checking for weeds.

Accounting, by contrast, is looking at the whole garden and deciding what to plant next season.
Without solid bookkeeping, accounting insights are unreliable — like reading a map with half the landmarks missing.

This chapter covers the three pillars of bookkeeping every business owner must master: recording transactions, reconciling accounts, and tracking expenses/receipts.

1. Recording Transactions

At its simplest, bookkeeping is just recording money in and money out. But the way you do it makes all the difference.
Cash vs Accrual Basis
- Cash Basis: You record revenue when cash is received and expenses when cash is paid. Simple and intuitive — great for freelancers or service businesses.
- Accrual Basis: You record revenue when earned (even if unpaid) and expenses when incurred (even if not yet paid).

- Provides a more accurate picture for growing businesses, especially those with inventory, contractors, or invoices.

Example: A graphic designer invoices a client in November, but the client pays in January.
- Cash basis: Revenue shows up in January.
- Accrual basis: Revenue shows up in November, when the work was done.

Most tax systems allow small businesses to use cash basis, but as soon as you want better insight (or bank loans), accrual often makes more sense.

Categories and Accounts
Every transaction belongs somewhere — rent, advertising, office supplies, meals, payroll. Your accounting system will use "accounts" (think folders) to group transactions. Categorization ensures your reports tell a meaningful story.

Mistake to avoid: Dumping everything into "Miscellaneous." You won't know later whether you overspent on marketing or rent.

Pro Tip #1: **NEVER** use "Miscellaneous" accounts, whether is income, expenses, liabilities, assets or any others.

Automation Helps
Modern systems like QuickBooks or Xero pull bank transactions daily. Instead of typing line by line, you just confirm or adjust categories. This saves hours and reduces errors.

Pro Tip #2: Set up "rules" so recurring expenses are automatically recognized, but **only for those transactions that are always posted into the same account**. For example, a payment to the electric company will always be posted to Utilities (with Electricity as sub-account); however, a purchase at Staples does not always get posted to Office Supplies because you can buy equipment and furniture.

2. Reconciling Accounts

Recording is step one, but reconciliation is what makes your books trustworthy. Reconciliation means comparing your records against actual bank or credit card statements to confirm they match.

Why It Matters
- Catches bank errors, double charges, or missed deposits.
- Ensures your cash balance is real — not inflated by uncleared checks or delayed deposits.
- Makes tax filing and financial reporting accurate.

Example: Your accounting system says you have $10,200 in the bank. Your actual statement says $9,800. Without reconciliation, you might think you have $400 more than reality — and overspend.

How Often?
At a minimum, reconcile monthly when statements arrive. Many businesses reconcile weekly for tighter cash control.

The Process

1. Pull your bank or credit card statement.
2. In your software, mark each transaction that appears on the statement.
3. Investigate differences:
   - o   A missing expense? Enter it.
   - o   A double entry? Delete it.
   - o   Bank fees not recorded? Add them.
4. Confirm ending balances match in your accounting software and your bank statements.

Pro Tip #3: Most modern systems offer "bank reconciliation" tools that make this process almost automatic. You click through matching transactions, and the software flags any discrepancies.

3. Tracking Expenses & Receipts

This is where many small businesses fall apart. Without proper expense tracking, you lose deductions, overpay taxes, and can't see where money leaks out.

Receipts: Old School vs New School

- Old School: Shoebox or manila folder stuffed with paper receipts. Works until you lose the folder or receipts fade.
- New School: Take a picture with your phone and upload it directly into your accounting system. Many apps extract vendor, date, and amount automatically.

Why It's Critical
- Tax savings: Every deductible expense reduces taxable income. If you don't track it, you're giving the government free money.
- Budget control: Helps you spot overspending (e.g., subscriptions you don't use).
- Audit defense: If the IRS or state tax authority asks for proof, digital receipts are gold.

Best Practices
- Separate business & personal finances. Always use a dedicated bank account and credit card. Mixing transactions makes bookkeeping a nightmare.
- Tag expenses properly. Meals, marketing, travel, office — don't leave things uncategorized or incorrectly posted into the wrong account.
- Review monthly. Scan reports to see spending patterns and catch errors early.

Pro Tip #4: Use expense-tracking as a management tool, not just compliance. Example: noticing your marketing spend went up 40% last quarter but sales didn't — time to adjust strategy.

Putting It Together
Bookkeeping may feel mundane, but it's the foundation of financial clarity. If you record diligently, reconcile consistently, and track expenses with discipline, you'll always know:
- How much cash is truly available.
- Whether you're profitable month to month.
- Where money is being wasted or well spent.

Good bookkeeping is like daily exercise — small, regular effort prevents bigger problems later. Many businesses don't fail because their idea was bad — they fail because they ran out of cash or didn't understand where it was going. Bookkeeping is the guardrail that keeps your business safely on the road.

Chapter 5 – Cash Flow Management

Why Cash Flow Is the Lifeblood of Your Business

Cash flow is the **movement of money in and out of your business**. Managing it well means ensuring that you always have enough cash to:

- Pay employees and contractors on time.
- Cover operating expenses like rent, utilities, and insurance.
- Purchase inventory or materials without panic.
- Invest in new opportunities without scrambling for financing.

Profits look nice on paper, but **cash pays the bills**. Many companies collapse not because they're unprofitable, but because they **ran out of cash at the wrong moment**.

In business, **cash is oxygen**. You can hold your breath without profit for a while — maybe you take on investment, maybe you run at a loss while building your market. But without cash in hand, the clock starts ticking toward shutdown almost immediately. That's because **profit measures performance over a set period**, while **cash flow measures liquidity at this very moment**.

Think of cash flow management as keeping fuel in your business's gas tank. Even a profitable company will stall if the tank runs dry.

This chapter covers three core skills: **forecasting cash needs, handling slow payments, and building a cash reserve.**

The Two Types of Cash Flow

Understanding whether you have **positive** or **negative** cash flow — and why — is the starting point of mastery.

1. **Positive Cash Flow** — More money is coming in than going out during a given period.
   This is the ideal position: you can pay bills, reinvest, save, and reward yourself.
   However, positive cash flow doesn't automatically mean the business is healthy — it could come from taking on debt rather than actual profitability.

2. **Negative Cash Flow** — More money is leaving the business than entering during the period.
   This can happen temporarily during a planned expansion or seasonal low, but if it continues, it signals serious operational or sales problems.

Pro Tip: Look at *patterns*, not just single months. Some businesses naturally have seasonal dips and spikes — a negative month in isolation doesn't mean failure, but a trend of negative cash flow will sink even profitable companies.

The Cash Flow Statement: Your Early Warning System
The Cash Flow Statement is one of the "big three" financial reports, but it deserves special attention here because it tells you **how your money actually moves** — something the P&L and Balance Sheet can't show directly.

It's divided into three main sections:

1. **Operating Activities** — Day-to-day business operations: customer payments received, payments made to suppliers, payroll, rent, taxes.
2. **Investing Activities** — Cash spent on or received from buying/selling long-term assets like property, equipment, or other businesses.
3. **Financing Activities** — Money borrowed, loans repaid, issuing shares, or withdrawing owner equity.

Why it matters:

- If your Operating Cash Flow is consistently negative, you're relying on financing or asset sales to stay afloat — not a sustainable situation.
- It reveals the timing of cash movement, which helps you anticipate and fix gaps.

Why Timing Is Everything

Even if you have profitable sales, **when** cash arrives is often more important than the total amount.

Timing issues create **cash flow gaps** — periods when you have expenses to pay before your income arrives.

Example Scenario:

- April 1: You send a $15,000 invoice to a corporate client with net-60 payment terms.
- April 10: Rent ($3,500) and payroll ($7,000) are due.
- April 20: You must pay $1,500 to suppliers for materials.

If you have only $5,000 in the bank, you're in trouble weeks before the client pays.

Solutions:

- Negotiate shorter payment terms (net-15 or net-30).
- Request deposits or progress payments for large jobs.
- Maintain a cash buffer for these gaps.

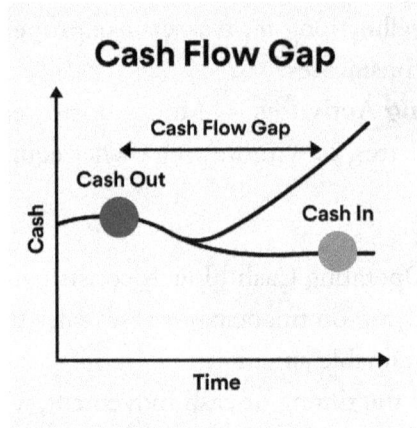

Figure: The Cash Flow Gap

A chart with two lines — one showing "Bills Due" and the other "Payments Received" — with a shaded gap between them representing a funding shortfall.

1. Forecasting Cash Needs

Forecasting is about looking ahead — not just reacting. It answers: *Will we have enough money to cover payroll, rent, and bills next month? What about three months from now?*

The Basics

- Start with your **opening cash balance** (what's in the bank today).
- Add **expected inflows** (customer payments, loan draws, investment funds).
- Subtract **expected outflows** (rent, payroll, utilities, supplier invoices, debt repayments, taxes).

- The result is your **projected ending balance**.

Example:
- Opening balance: $15,000
- Inflows (customer payments due): $20,000
- Outflows (payroll, rent, bills): $25,000
- Projected ending balance: $10,000

This quick snapshot tells you whether you'll be safe or scrambling.

How Far to Forecast
- **Small service businesses:** Forecast 1–3 months ahead.
- **Product or inventory-heavy businesses:** Forecast at least 6–12 months since inventory ties up cash longer.
- **Fast-growth companies:** Update forecasts weekly — growth burns cash faster than expected.

Pro Tips:
- **Include seasonality.** If sales drop every August, plan for it.
- **Don't forget irregular expenses.** Insurance premiums, tax deadlines, or annual subscriptions often sneak up and wreck cash flow.
- **Stress-test.** Build scenarios: *What if sales drop 20%? What if a big client pays late?*

Forecasting isn't about predicting the future perfectly — it's about spotting problems early enough to act.

2. Handling Slow Payments

One of the biggest cash flow killers isn't overspending — it's customers who don't pay on time. A great sales month is meaningless if invoices linger unpaid for 60–90 days.

Preventive Strategies

- **Clear terms upfront.** Always include payment terms (e.g., Net 15, Net 30) on invoices.
- **Deposit or upfront payment.** For projects, ask for 25–50% upfront. This lowers your risk.
- **Automated invoicing.** Send invoices immediately, not weeks later. Delayed billing means delayed cash.
- **Payment Methods.** Accept multiple payment methods, including credit card, ACH, and online platforms.

Follow-Up System

- Send a **friendly reminder** a few days before the due date.
- Follow up **immediately** after the due date with a professional but firm reminder.
- For chronic late payers, shorten terms or require prepayment.

Example:
You invoice $5,000 due in 30 days. With reminders on day 25 and day 31, you get paid on day 33 instead of day 60. Over time, this discipline can cut weeks off your cash cycle.

Incentives and Penalties
- Offer **small discounts** for early payment (e.g., 2% off if paid within 10 days).
- Charge **late fees** if terms are ignored (and enforce them consistently).

Pro Tip: Watch your **Accounts Receivable Aging Report** monthly. It shows which invoices are overdue and by how long. Many businesses fail not because they lack sales, but because cash is locked in unpaid invoices.

3. Building a Cash Reserve

Even with forecasting and collection discipline, surprises happen — a key client delays payment, equipment fails, or sales dip unexpectedly. That's why every business needs a **cash cushion.**

Cash reserves are your financial shock absorbers.
Aim for at least one to three months of operating expenses saved in an account you don't touch for everyday spending.

Benefits:
- Smooths over seasonal slowdowns.
- Buys time if a major client pays late.
- Allows you to seize quick opportunities without outside funding.

How Much to Save
- Aim for **2–3 months of operating expenses** as a baseline.
- For volatile industries, 4–6 months is safer.

Example: If your average monthly expenses are $30,000, your cash
reserve target is $60,000–$90,000.

How to Build It
- **Start small.** Set aside 5–10% of monthly profits until
  reserves grow.
- **Treat it like a bill.** Transfer cash into a separate "rainy
  day" account regularly.
- **Use windfalls wisely.** Tax refunds, unexpected profits,
  or one-time bonuses should boost reserves first.

When to Use It
- Cover short-term gaps (like bridging payroll until
  receivables clear).
- Handle true emergencies (equipment breakdowns,
  economic shocks).
- **Not** for avoidable overspending — if reserves are bailing
  you out every month, you have a budgeting problem.

Delay Payables (Ethically)
Take full advantage of vendor payment terms without damaging
relationships. If you have net-30 terms, pay on day 29 — not on
day 5.

Bonus: Align payables with your receivables. If you get paid by
customers on the 15th and 30th, aim to schedule major payables
right after those dates.

Control Spending

Review your expenses monthly and cut anything that doesn't contribute directly to revenue or operational efficiency.

Common Cash Flow Pitfalls

- **Over-reliance on credit** — Using debt to cover everyday operating expenses is a warning sign.
- **Overstocking inventory** — Money tied up in unsold goods is money you can't use elsewhere.
- **Ignoring seasonal patterns** — Failing to prepare for low months creates unnecessary panic.
- **Mixing personal and business funds** — Makes tracking cash flow nearly impossible.
- **No regular monitoring** — Reviewing cash flow only quarterly means problems fester.

Practical tip:

Print your last 90 days of bank statements and highlight every expense in one of three colors:

- **Green:** Must-have to operate.
- **Yellow:** Nice to have — can reduce or delay.
- **Red:** Not needed — cut it.

Putting It All Together

Cash flow management isn't glamorous, but it's the difference between a business that struggles paycheck to paycheck and one that grows with confidence.

- **Forecasting** gives you visibility.
- **Collections discipline** turns sales into real cash.
- **Reserves** give you peace of mind and staying power.

The best-run companies treat cash flow like oxygen: always monitored, never taken for granted. Get this right, and you

won't just survive tough months — you'll have the stability to
seize opportunities others can't afford.

Chapter 6 – End-of-Month and Year-End Checklists

Accounting isn't just about recording transactions as they happen — it's about **closing the loop on your finances** so that your numbers don't just exist but actually mean something. Each month, bills get paid, customers send in payments, payroll runs, and countless small transactions take place. Unless you pause at regular intervals to make sure everything is captured and reconciled, your financial picture becomes blurry and unreliable.

Many business owners make the mistake of pushing bookkeeping to the background, thinking they'll "catch up at tax time." The result? A frantic scramble at year-end with missing receipts, unexplained charges, uncollected invoices, and reports that don't add up. By then, it's too late to make meaningful decisions — you're left cleaning up the past instead of steering the future.

That's why successful businesses treat accounting like **a discipline, not an afterthought.** They use two structured processes:

1. The Monthly Close Checklist

   A short, repeatable routine that ensures your records are accurate as of the end of each month. This includes reconciling accounts, reviewing payables and receivables, checking payroll, and updating forecasts. Done consistently, it keeps your books in shape and gives you reliable numbers for decision-making in real time.

2. The Year-End Checklist

A deeper, more comprehensive process that prepares your business for taxes, compliance, and strategic planning. This includes final reconciliations, inventory counts, asset depreciation, and preparing employee and contractor reports. Year-end is when your books need to stand up to outside scrutiny — whether that's your CPA, lenders, investors, or even a tax auditor.

Think of these processes in terms of personal health:

- **Monthly closes are like brushing and flossing.** They're simple, routine habits that keep your financial "teeth" healthy.
- **Year-end closes are like a full dental exam.** They go deeper, looking for hidden issues, cleaning up what you might have missed, and making sure everything is strong for the year ahead.

Skip the small habits, and the big exam becomes painful — expensive, stressful, and sometimes damaging. But if you maintain a monthly rhythm, the year-end process becomes straightforward, even empowering. Instead of dreading tax season, you'll enter it with confidence, knowing your numbers are solid, your risks are covered, and your business is prepared for growth.

End-of-Month Checklist

At the end of each month, your primary goal is to confirm that **your books match reality** — your bank balances, credit card activity, payroll records, and vendor/customer transactions should all align. This process not only keeps your numbers accurate but also prevents small mistakes from compounding into major financial headaches.

Step 1: Reconcile Bank and Credit Card Accounts
- **Match every transaction** in your accounting system to your bank and credit card statements. Don't just rely on your accounting software — go line by line.
- Watch for:
  - **Missing deposits** (e.g., a client payment was received but never recorded).
  - **Duplicate charges** (sometimes vendors accidentally charge twice).
  - **Unauthorized transactions** (fraudulent charges or errors).
- Reconciliation ensures you aren't relying on "phantom balances" that look good on paper but don't exist in your actual account.

Tip: Cloud accounting systems like QuickBooks, Xero, or Wave often import transactions automatically via bank feeds. That makes reconciliation easier, but **automation doesn't mean accuracy.** You still need to review and approve each entry.

Example: If your books show $15,000 in your operating account but your reconciled bank balance is $12,700, you may have unrecorded checks or delayed deposits. That's a $2,300 reality gap you need to address before making spending decisions.

Step 2: Review Accounts Receivable (A/R)
- Run an **Aging Report** to see who owes you money and how long invoices have been outstanding.

- Take action:
  - Follow up on 30-, 60-, and 90-day overdue invoices.
  - Offer payment plans if needed, but avoid letting balances sit indefinitely.
- Flag doubtful accounts for potential write-offs or collection efforts.

Why it matters: Uncollected revenue is one of the biggest killers of small business cash flow. Staying proactive ensures you turn sales into actual cash.

Example: If you have $25,000 in receivables, but $18,000 is more than 60 days overdue, your "real" cash position is far weaker than it looks.

Step 3: Review Accounts Payable (A/P)

- List all bills coming due in the next 30–60 days.
- Verify that vendor invoices are entered correctly (double-check amounts, dates, and vendor details).
- Schedule payments strategically:
  - Don't pay so early that you drain working capital.
  - Don't pay so late that you damage vendor relationships or incur late fees.

Best practice: If your vendor offers a small early-payment discount (e.g., "2/10, net 30"), compare the effective savings against the benefit of holding onto the cash longer.

Step 4: Record Payroll and Related Taxes

- Verify payroll entries: wages, withholdings, employer taxes, and benefits.
- Ensure all tax filings (federal, state, and local) are submitted on time. Penalties for missed payroll taxes are some of the most severe a small business can face.

Tip: If you use a payroll service, don't assume everything is error-free. Spot-check pay stubs and confirm tax remittances.

Step 5: Review Expense Categorization

- Double-check that expenses are coded correctly:
  o Office expenses vs. office supplies.
  o Travel vs. meals & entertainment.
  o Subscriptions vs. professional services.
- Proper categorization:
  o Helps with accurate budgeting.
  o Ensures you don't miss tax deductions.
  o Keeps your reports meaningful.

Example: Misclassifying a $500 professional software license as "office supplies" may not break your books, but if repeated, it could distort expense patterns and lead you to make poor budget decisions.

Step 6: Update Cash Flow Forecast

- Take your forecast for the upcoming months and **update it with actual inflows and outflows.**
- Compare projections to reality: Are you ahead of plan, or falling behind?
- Spot shortfalls early so you can adjust (delay discretionary spending, speed up collections, or arrange short-term financing).

Best practice: Even a simple spreadsheet that projects 13 weeks of cash can be a powerful planning tool.

Step 7: Generate and Review Financial Reports

At a minimum, run and actually read these three core reports:

1. **Profit & Loss (P&L):** Did you operate at a profit this month? Are there any unusual expense spikes?
2. **Balance Sheet:** Do assets, liabilities, and equity line up with your expectations? Any unexpected liabilities?
3. **Cash Flow Statement:** Is your cash position trending up or down, and why?

The point isn't just to produce reports — it's to **interpret them.** Numbers don't speak on their own; they require a narrative.

Example: A positive P&L doesn't necessarily mean you're in good shape. You could be profitable on paper but still running into cash shortages if customers are slow to pay. Reviewing all three reports together gives the full picture.

Bottom line: The end-of-month close is about control. It ensures that your numbers reflect reality, giving you confidence in decisions like hiring, investing in growth, or managing debt. Skip it, and you're flying blind.

Year-End Checklist

Monthly closes keep your financial house tidy, but the **year-end close** is the equivalent of deep cleaning: preparing your books for taxes, compliance, and strategic planning. Think of it as a bridge between one fiscal year and the next — ensuring you end strong and start fresh.

Step 1: Confirm All Transactions Are Entered

- Go line by line and make sure every **income and expense item** is recorded. Even small omissions can distort your bottom line.
- Pay special attention to **December transactions** — year-end can be chaotic, and expenses like annual software renewals, holiday bonuses, or supplier bills often slip through the cracks.
- Cross-check your accounting system against:
  o Bank statements
  o Credit card statements
  o Vendor invoices
  o Payroll records

Example: If you forget to record a $2,000 year-end bonus paid to staff, your net income will be overstated. That not only skews profitability but also leads to an unpleasant surprise at tax time.

Step 2: Reconcile All Accounts

Monthly reconciliation is good; year-end reconciliation is **non-negotiable.**

- Go beyond bank accounts — reconcile:
  o Loans (balance should match lender statements)
  o Credit cards
  o Merchant accounts (Stripe, PayPal, Square)
  o Petty cash (count the actual bills in the drawer!)

- Confirm that your books **match every external statement**. Any discrepancies should be investigated before filing taxes.

Tip: Merchant processors often take fees off the top. If you only record gross deposits, your income and expenses will both be wrong.

Step 3: Inventory Count (if applicable)
- Conduct a **physical inventory count** at year-end. Don't just rely on your software — do a manual check.
- Record adjustments for shrinkage (theft), spoilage (expired goods), or miscounts.
- Reconcile your counted inventory with your accounting system to ensure your balance sheet reflects reality.

Why it matters: An overstated inventory inflates your assets and net income. For product businesses, this step is critical for both accurate taxes and financial clarity.

Step 4: Fixed Assets and Depreciation
- Record all **capital asset purchases** made during the year — equipment, vehicles, furniture, computers, etc.
- Update **depreciation schedules** so you capture the correct expense for the year.
- Dispose of assets that are no longer in use. If you sold or scrapped equipment, record the disposal to keep your asset list clean.

Example: A small construction company buys a $25,000 truck in July. If they forget to add it to fixed assets and start depreciation, they miss out on a significant tax deduction.

Step 5: Review Outstanding Receivables and Payables
- Review your Accounts Receivable Aging Report and **make one last push** to collect overdue invoices before year-end.
- Review Accounts Payable and plan which bills to pay before Dec 31. Paying down high-interest obligations can save interest expense in the new year.
- Consider cash vs. accrual tax implications:
  - On a cash basis? Collect receivables early to boost income this year or delay billing until January to defer income.
  - On an accrual basis? Ensure all bills and invoices are recorded in the proper year.

Tip: Don't carry dead receivables forward forever. Discuss potential write-offs with your CPA.

Step 6: Employee & Contractor Reporting
- **Employees (W-2s):** Verify that wages, taxes, and benefits are correctly recorded. Confirm addresses and Social Security Numbers before filing deadlines.
- **Contractors (1099s in the U.S.):** Collect W-9 forms and confirm Taxpayer IDs (TIN/EIN).
- Missing or incorrect data in January creates last-minute panic and risks IRS penalties.

Pro tip: Many payroll platforms will generate W-2s and 1099s automatically if you input accurate data ahead of time. Do a data check now, not in January.

Step 7: Tax Preparation

This is where you shift into compliance mode. Organize all supporting documentation:

- Bank and credit card statements
- Loan agreements and amortization schedules
- Asset purchase receipts
- Payroll tax filings (941s, state filings, etc.)
- Sales tax records

Schedule a **year-end meeting with your CPA** to:

- Review deductions and credits
- Adjust estimated tax payments
- Discuss any year-end tax strategies (e.g., Section 179 deductions, retirement contributions, charitable donations).

Why it matters: A one-hour CPA meeting in December can save thousands of dollars in April.

Step 8: Strategic Review

Year-end isn't just about taxes — it's about **insight and planning.**

- Compare actual results to your budget and forecasts. Where did you outperform? Where did you fall short?
- Identify your most profitable customers, services, or products.
- Review trends: margins, cash flow, and growth trajectory.

- Set financial goals for the next year — and link them to operational initiatives.

Example: If 70% of your profit came from one service line but you spent most of your time chasing low-margin work, it may be time to **double down on your winners.**

Bottom line: The year-end close isn't just about compliance — it's about clarity. It gives you a clean slate, accurate numbers for tax filings, and the strategic insights to start the new year with confidence.

The Big Picture

Closing the books isn't just a bookkeeping ritual — it's the backbone of business survival and growth.

Monthly Closes: The Pulse of Your Business

Monthly closes are like checking your vital signs. They give you an accurate read on:

- **Cash position** — Do you have enough to cover payroll, rent, and upcoming bills?
- **Profitability** — Are you making money, or are expenses creeping ahead of revenue?
- **Trends** — Is sales growth steady, seasonal, or declining?

By reconciling accounts, reviewing receivables, and generating reports monthly, you keep your financials clean and actionable. This regular cadence makes it possible to **spot problems early** — before they snowball.

Example: A restaurant that waits until year-end to notice food costs rising by 15% may lose tens of thousands in profit. One that closes monthly catches the issue by March, renegotiates vendor contracts, and protects its margins.

Year-End Closes: The Reset Button

While monthly closes keep the heart beating, year-end closes are like a full physical exam. They don't just tell you if you survived the year — they set you up for the year ahead.

- **Tax readiness:** Accurate books reduce stress during tax filing, lower audit risk, and ensure you claim every legitimate deduction.
- **Audit protection:** Clean records demonstrate credibility to lenders, investors, or regulators.
- **Strategic planning:** Year-end closes reveal which customers, services, or products drove profitability — insights you can use to set next year's strategy.

Example: A marketing agency discovers, through its year-end review, that 80% of its profits came from only two clients. That knowledge helps them refocus their sales efforts on similar high-value clients instead of chasing low-margin projects.

.

The Cost of Skipping the Close

Businesses that fail to close consistently end up in **reaction mode**:

- Scrambling at tax time, handing their CPA a shoebox of receipts.
- Making decisions based on gut feelings instead of hard numbers.
- Missing growth opportunities because they can't see which parts of the business are working.
- Losing credibility with banks or investors when asked for up-to-date financials.
- Equity balances show incorrect numbers (balance sheet items carry over with time and remain on the statement).

Imagine: You're considering a loan to expand, but your books are six months behind. The bank asks for financials, and you can't provide accurate numbers. Expansion stalls — not because your business isn't strong, but because your accounting isn't.

Closing the Books = Business Survival

Ultimately, the close isn't busywork. It's not about perfection or satisfying your accountant. It's about running a business with **eyes wide open**:

- So you know where you stand today.
- So you can anticipate tomorrow.
- So you can grow with confidence instead of guessing.

Businesses that commit to monthly and year-end closes **operate from a place of clarity.** Those that don't? They run blind — until something breaks.

Bottom line: Closing the books is more than accounting hygiene. It's the discipline that separates businesses that struggle to survive from those that thrive and scale.

Chapter 7 – Taxes Made Simple

Taxes don't have to feel like rocket science.

For many small business owners, though, they do. The word alone can trigger a stress response: visions of complicated forms, intimidating notices from the IRS, and the feeling that one wrong move could bring disaster. It's no wonder that, year after year, business owners put off dealing with taxes until the last possible moment.

Here's the reality: most of the pain comes not from the taxes themselves but from the **way we approach them**.

- **Reactive vs. proactive.** Too many entrepreneurs wait until April to even think about their tax situation. By then, it's too late to make smart decisions—you're stuck with the past twelve months, no matter how messy they are.
- **Paper chaos.** Receipts in shoeboxes, invoices spread across email threads, half-complete spreadsheets, and a bank account that doesn't quite reconcile. Sound familiar? This isn't a tax problem—it's a workflow problem.
- **Memory gaps.** Ever try to recall what that $428 charge from last May was? Without a system, you spend hours piecing together transactions instead of running your business.
- **Dependence on others.** Many owners feel at the mercy of their accountant, terrified of the final number they'll hear once everything is filed.

But it doesn't have to be that way.

With the right system, taxes become **predictable, manageable, and even strategic**. Instead of a yearly scramble, they become part of the rhythm of your business—the same way you check your bank balance or review your sales.

- **Predictable**: You know roughly what you'll owe each quarter, and you've set the money aside.
- **Manageable**: Your records are organized, digital, and easy to pull when needed.
- **Strategic**: You're not just minimizing your tax bill— you're aligning tax planning with your growth goals, retirement savings, and reinvestment decisions.

This chapter is about transforming how you think about taxes. Not as a burden, but as a **tool**—one that, when used properly, can:

- Reduce costs by uncovering legitimate deductions you might miss.
- Avoid ugly surprises by spreading out payments instead of facing a giant April bill.
- Support better business decisions by showing you the true, after-tax impact of your choices.

And here's the promise: we'll keep it in **plain English**. No drowning in IRS jargon, no unnecessary complexity. By the end, you'll know what actually matters, what doesn't, and how to stay ahead of taxes without burning out.

Think of this chapter as your guide to going from **tax panic mode** to **tax confident mode**—where taxes are no longer an annual nightmare but simply another part of running a smart, resilient business.

1. Why Taxes Feel Overwhelming

For most small business owners, taxes aren't inherently complicated—it's the *experience* that feels overwhelming. Here's why:

Too many moving parts.
When people hear "taxes," they often lump everything together into one big headache. But in reality, there are different categories of taxes, each with its own rules and due dates:

- **Income taxes** (federal and state) that you pay on your profits.
- **Payroll taxes** for employees, which involve withholdings, employer matches, and timely filings.
- **Sales tax** collected on customer transactions, varying by state or even county.
- **Self-employment tax** if you're a sole proprietor or single-member LLC.

It feels endless because it's fragmented—like juggling four balls while trying to balance on one foot. Without a system, deadlines sneak up, and suddenly you're behind.

Mindset shift: Think of taxes not as "everything at once," but as a **set of smaller, recurring tasks**. Once you know which ones apply to your business, you can put them on autopilot with calendars, reminders, or accounting software.

Uncertainty

One of the biggest stressors is the mystery factor: *"What am I going to owe?"* You don't know until your accountant crunches the numbers, and that lack of visibility can feel like waiting for a pop quiz you never studied for.

This uncertainty often comes from not keeping books current. If you don't know your monthly profit, you won't know your annual tax liability.

Solution: By maintaining monthly closes (see Chapter 6), you'll always have a near-real-time picture of your taxable income. Instead of waiting until April, you'll see trends forming throughout the year and can adjust—whether that means saving more cash for taxes or reinvesting in deductible expenses before year-end.

Poor habits.

Let's be honest: many business owners treat taxes like laundry—ignore it until the pile is unbearable, then tackle it in a single exhausting weekend. Waiting until tax season to organize receipts, invoices, and expenses almost guarantees chaos.

Common habits that cause problems:
- Throwing receipts in a shoebox (or worse, the trash).
- Ignoring small expenses because they feel insignificant.
- Mixing personal and business transactions in the same bank account.

These habits don't just waste time—they cost money. Missed deductions add up, and poor records make audits more painful.

Fix: Build **micro-habits**. Snap a photo of receipts on your phone and upload them weekly. Use a separate business checking account and card. Categorize expenses as you go instead of "catching up later." Small, consistent habits save dozens of hours (and thousands of dollars) at tax time.

Fear of Mistakes

Even confident entrepreneurs can feel intimidated by the IRS or their state tax agency. The idea of a penalty, an audit, or a scary letter in the mail is enough to cause paralysis.

The fear is real, but here's the truth: most penalties aren't about fraud—they're about simple errors like filing late, underpaying estimates, or forgetting to remit payroll tax. These are fixable with better systems.

Reframe: Think of tax agencies less like monsters and more like referees. Their job is to make sure the game is played fairly. If your books are clean and you follow the rules, there's nothing to fear.

The Bottom Line:

Taxes are just a **reflection of your business activity**. If you keep your books clean, track income and expenses consistently, and understand the basics, filing becomes a matter of reporting—not scrambling.

2. The Big Three Taxes Every Business Faces

While tax codes vary across states and industries, most small business owners in the U.S. consistently deal with three main categories of taxes: income taxes, payroll taxes, and sales taxes. Understanding these isn't just about compliance—it's about avoiding costly mistakes and knowing where to save money.

Income Taxes

Income taxes are the most familiar—and the most misunderstood. The key thing to remember is that you are taxed on profits, not revenue.

Example: If you brought in $100,000 in sales but spent $70,000 on expenses (rent, payroll, supplies, software, etc.), you're taxed only on the remaining $30,000 profit. That's why diligent expense tracking directly lowers your tax bill.

But how those profits get taxed depends entirely on your business structure:

- **Sole Proprietorship / Single-Member LLC**
  Profits "pass through" directly to your personal tax return
- on **Schedule C**. You'll also pay **self-employment tax** (15.3% for Social Security and Medicare) in addition to income tax. Many first-time entrepreneurs are shocked by this because it's much higher than what they paid as employees.
- **Partnership / Multi-Member LLC**
  The business itself doesn't pay taxes; instead, it files an informational return and issues each partner a

- **Schedule K-1**. Partners then report their share of profits on personal returns, regardless of whether the money was actually distributed. This is where "phantom income" surprises some owners—you may owe taxes even if you kept profits inside the business.
- **S-Corporation**
This is still a pass-through entity, but it can reduce self-employment taxes. Owners typically pay themselves a "reasonable salary" (subject to payroll taxes) and then take additional profits as distributions, which aren't subject to self-employment tax. It's more paperwork but can save thousands once profits exceed ~$40,000–$50,000.
- **C-Corporation**
A C-Corp pays its own taxes at the corporate rate (currently 21%). If profits are distributed as dividends, owners pay taxes again at the personal level ("double taxation"). That said, C-corps can make sense for companies that want to reinvest heavily, attract investors, or offer stock options.

Key takeaway: The right structure can dramatically impact your tax bill. For some businesses, switching from sole proprietorship to S-Corp can save $10,000+ per year in self-employment taxes.

Payroll Taxes
If you have employees (or even if you pay yourself a salary in an S-Corp), payroll taxes become unavoidable. They're not optional, and missing deadlines here can sink a business fast.

You're responsible for:

- **Withholding** federal and state income tax, Social Security, and Medicare from employee paychecks.
- **Paying the employer's share** of Social Security and Medicare (currently 7.65% on wages up to the annual cap).
- **Filing quarterly reports** (like Form 941 in the U.S.) and making timely deposits to the IRS and state agencies.

Why it matters: Payroll taxes aren't your money—they're trust funds you hold for the government. If you withhold from employees but fail to remit, the IRS treats it as theft. Penalties are severe and can pierce the corporate veil, making you personally liable.

Pro tip: Don't run payroll manually unless you're an accountant. Use a Payroll Service Provider to handle calculations, filings, and deposits automatically. They're worth every penny compared to the risk of mistakes.

Sales Taxes

Sales taxes are a tricky beast because they vary not just by state, but sometimes by **county, city, or even product category**.

- If you sell **tangible goods** (like retail products), you almost certainly need to collect sales tax where your business has a physical presence.
- If you sell **services**, rules vary widely—some states tax them, others don't.
- If you sell **online**, the 2018 Supreme Court case *South Dakota v. Wayfair* changed the game. Now, states can

- require you to collect sales tax even if you don't have a physical office there, as long as you cross certain sales thresholds ("economic nexus").

Example: If you sell $120,000 worth of products to customers in Texas, you may be required to register for a Texas sales tax permit and remit taxes there—even if you're based in another state.

Pro tip: Don't guess. Use software or an accountant to automatically calculate and remit the correct rates.

Warning: Missing payroll or sales tax filings is deadly. Unlike income tax (where you might negotiate with your CPA or IRS), payroll and sales taxes generate **automatic penalties and interest** that rack up quickly. In extreme cases, the IRS can freeze your accounts.

Best Practice: Automate as much as possible. Let payroll software or provider handle paychecks and filings. Let sales tax software, or your accountant, calculate rates and file returns. Your job is to monitor, not manually manage.

The Bottom Line:

Mastering the "big three" isn't about becoming a tax expert. It's about setting up systems so income taxes, payroll taxes, and sales taxes happen on schedule—without surprises. Do that, and you'll never feel like taxes are controlling your business again.

3. The Self-Employment Tax Trap

Most first-time business owners expect to pay income tax on their profits. What often catches them off guard is the self-employment tax — a 15.3% tax that covers Social Security and Medicare.

When you're an employee, you only see half of this tax come out of your paycheck (7.65%). Your employer quietly pays the other half on your behalf. But when you're self-employed, you're both the employee and the employer. That means you're responsible for the full 15.3%.

How It Works (Example)
Let's say you're a sole proprietor and your business earns $60,000 in profit after expenses.
- You'll owe income tax on that $60,000 (based on your personal tax bracket).
- On top of that, you'll owe self-employment tax:
  - $60,000 \times 15.3\% = \$9,180$

So even before paying income tax, nearly $10,000 of your profit goes to Social Security and Medicare.

This often surprises entrepreneurs who thought they'd only be taxed once. It's one of the biggest reasons new business owners feel like the money is "gone" faster than expected.

Why This Matters
- **Cash Flow Shock**: Many business owners don't set aside enough throughout the year. April rolls around, and they're blindsided by a $10K+ bill.

- **Quarterly Tax Payments**: If you expect to owe more than $1,000, the IRS requires you to pay estimated taxes **four times a year**. Miss them, and you'll face penalties.
- **Scaling Costs**: As profits rise, so does the tax burden. At $100K profit, self-employment tax alone is $15,300 — not counting income tax.

How to Manage the Trap
1. **Plan Ahead**
   o A good rule of thumb is to set aside **25–30% of your profits** in a separate savings account for taxes. That way, you're never caught short.
   o Use apps like QuickBooks, Wave, or Tax Planner Pro to calculate and track estimates.
2. **Consider Your Business Structure**
   o **Sole Proprietorship / Single-Member LLC**: Simple and cheap to set up, but exposes you to the full self-employment (SE) tax.
   o **S-Corporation**: Often a smart move once you're earning consistent profits (usually $40K+). You pay yourself a reasonable salary (subject to payroll tax) and then take additional profits as distributions, which aren't subject to the 15.3%. This can save thousands annually.
   o Example: If your business earns $80,000:
   ▪ As a sole proprietor, you'd pay SE tax on all $80K = $12,240.
   ▪ As an S-Corp owner, you might pay yourself a $45,000 salary (SE tax applies) and take $35,000 as distributions (no SE tax). That cuts your self-employment tax nearly in half.

3. Work With an accountant

- o   Not every business should become an S-Corp. It depends on your profit level, industry, and whether you plan to reinvest earnings.
- o   An accountant can run the numbers to see if the tax savings outweigh the added payroll and compliance costs.

o

Warning: Don't Play Games With Salaries

The IRS watches S-Corp owners closely. If you try to pay yourself a $10K salary and take $90K as distributions, they'll likely reclassify part of it as wages and hit you with penalties. Always set a reasonable salary for your role.

Bottom Line:

Self-employment tax is one of the biggest financial shocks for solo entrepreneurs. But with smart planning—setting aside money, making quarterly payments, and considering structures like S-Corps—you can turn the surprise into a **manageable, predictable part of doing business**. Done right, tax season stops being a panic and starts being just another line item in your business plan.

4. Staying Ahead with Quarterly Taxes

Most small business owners think about taxes once a year — usually in a panic. But the IRS (and most states) actually want you to **pay as you go.**

If you're self-employed or run a small business, you're required to pay **estimated taxes every quarter** if you expect to owe more than $1,000 at year-end. Miss them, and you'll face both penalties and interest.

Why Quarterly Taxes Exist

When you're an employee, your employer withholds income tax and payroll tax from every paycheck, then sends it to the IRS for you. The government gets their money all year long.

When you're self-employed, no one is withholding. So the IRS expects you to do it yourself — in four installments. Think of it as sending in "mini tax returns" throughout the year.

The Big Dates (U.S. Deadlines)

- **April 15** → Covers income from Jan–Mar
- **June 15** → Covers income from Apr–May
- **Sept 15** → Covers income from Jun–Aug
- **Jan 15 (next year)** → Covers income from Sep–Dec

Miss these dates? The IRS will happily tack on penalties — even if you pay the full amount when filing your return in April.

How to Estimate What You Owe

There are two common approaches:

1. **The Safe Harbor Method**
   - Pay **100% of last year's tax liability** (110% if your income was over $150,000).
   - This guarantees no penalties, even if you end up making way more this year.
   - Example: If you owed $12,000 last year, just send $3,000 each quarter this year.
2. **The Actual Income Method**

- o Estimate your current year's income and pay **as you go**.
- o Better for cash flow, but riskier if your estimates are too low.
- o Example: If you earn $20,000 profit in Q1, you might set aside ~30% ($6,000) and send it in.

Most owners use a mix: Safe Harbor to avoid penalties, then adjust if profits rise or fall.

Why This Matters for Business Owners

- **Cash Flow Discipline**. Quarterly taxes force you to set aside money regularly. No more "spending it all" and then panicking at year-end.
- **No Surprises**. If you're paying quarterly, your April filing is mostly paperwork, not a giant check.
- **Avoids Penalties**. Late or underpaid estimates mean unnecessary costs that eat into profits.

Pro Tips to Make Quarterly Taxes Painless

- **Open a "Tax Savings" Account**: Each month, move **25–30% of your profit** into a separate bank account. That way, when quarterly payments are due, the money's already there.
- **Automate Your Payments**: Use the IRS EFTPS system or your state's online portal. Schedule payments in advance so you don't miss deadlines. You can also automate your quarterly tax payments by instructing the IRS and State (if applicable) to take

- the payment directly from your bank account when you file your tax return. Discuss that option with your tax accountant.
- **Check In Mid-Year**: If your income jumps or dips, recalculate your estimates so you're not overpaying or underpaying.

Example Scenario
- You earn $80,000 in profit this year.
- You set aside 25% = $20,000 for taxes.
- Instead of waiting until April and owing a lump sum, you send **$5,000 each quarter**.
- At tax filing, if you slightly overpaid, you'll get a refund. If you underpaid, you'll only owe the difference — no penalties.

Bottom Line: Quarterly taxes aren't a punishment — they're a system to help you spread out the burden. Treat them like "business bills" that keep you compliant and stress-free. Handle them right, and tax season becomes nothing more than a formality.

5. The Power of Good Recordkeeping

If taxes feel overwhelming, it's usually not because the tax forms are impossible. It's because the **records behind them are a mess.**

Good recordkeeping is the difference between a calm (and possibly planned) tax season and a frantic one.

Think of your records as the **foundation of your financial house**. If they're solid, your tax return is quick, accurate, and defensible in an audit. If they're shaky, everything built on top of them — your deductions, your financial reports, even your ability to get loans — starts to crumble.

Why Recordkeeping Matters

1. **Accuracy**
   - Taxes are just a reflection of what already happened. If your income and expenses are recorded correctly, filing becomes straightforward.
   - Example: If you forget to log $2,000 in office supplies, you'll overpay tax because the IRS thinks you earned more profit than you did.

2. **Compliance**
   - The IRS and state agencies can audit up to 3 years back (sometimes longer). If they ask for receipts or documentation, you need to produce them.
   - A shoebox of crumpled papers doesn't cut it — clean records protect you.

3. **Financial Insight**
   - Records aren't just for taxes — they tell you how your business is really doing.
   - Example: By categorizing expenses, you may realize you're spending 20% of revenue on software subscriptions — and can trim costs.

4. **Peace of Mind**
   o When everything is tracked, you don't lie awake in March wondering what you forgot. You already know.

What "Good Records" Actually Look Like

- **Bank-Feed Accounting**: Use software that connects directly to your bank and credit cards (QuickBooks, Xero, Wave). Every transaction is imported automatically.
- **Receipt Capture**: Use apps or even your phone's camera. Snap the receipt and attach it to the transaction. No more lost paper trails.
- **Categorization Rules**: Set up your software so recurring expenses (like Zoom, Dropbox, or rent) are auto-recognized. Saves hours each month.
  o **Pro Tip**: We don't recommend auto-categorizing transactions. You should always see what transactions the bank and credit card are feeding your accounting software, and you are always aware of what comes out. If you auto-categorize, you won't see if there are duplicate charges, unauthorized charges, etc.
- **Separate Business & Personal Accounts**: Never mix. A clean business account makes bookkeeping almost effortless.
- **Monthly Close Routine**: Reconcile accounts every month. If you wait until year-end, it's ten times harder.

Example of the Cost of Bad Records

- A business owner makes $150,000 in sales and has $90,000 in expenses.
- But they failed to record $10,000 in receipts for supplies and travel.
- At a 25% tax rate, that mistake costs **$2,500 in extra taxes.**
- Add in interest and penalties if the IRS discovers it, and the real cost can exceed $4,000.

Poor records don't just create stress — they drain your bank account.

Practical Habits to Build Now

1. **Schedule a Weekly "Money Hour"**
   - Once a week, review your income, expenses, and bank feeds. Keep the habit small but consistent.
2. **Digitize Everything**
   - Keep electronic copies of invoices, contracts, and receipts. Cloud storage is safer than a filing cabinet. However, consider a local backup.
3. **Use Categories that Match Your Tax Return**
   - Align expense categories with IRS Schedule C (or your business structure's return). That way, your software reports flow directly into your tax forms.
4. **Don't Wait Until April**
   - If you only update records once a year, you're not just making tax season painful — you're flying blind all year long.

The Audit-Proof Mindset

Always ask yourself:

"If the IRS asked me to prove this expense, could I do it in 30 seconds?"

If the answer is yes — you're safe. If not, fix your system.

Bottom Line: Good recordkeeping isn't about being a neat freak. It's about saving money, reducing stress, and running your business with confidence. Think of it as the cheapest form of insurance you can buy — insurance against mistakes, penalties, and sleepless nights.

6. Deductions: What You Can (and Can't) Write Off

For many entrepreneurs, deductions are the most confusing part of taxes — and the most powerful. A deduction reduces your taxable income, which in turn reduces the taxes you owe. But the IRS isn't handing out freebies. The golden rule is:

Expenses must be "ordinary and necessary" for running your business.

- **Ordinary** = Common in your trade or industry.
- **Necessary** = Helpful and appropriate for your business (even if not absolutely essential).

The "Can Write Off" Category (Legitimate Deductions)

Here are common (and often overlooked) deductions that small business owners should track:

1. **Home Office Deduction**
    o If you regularly and exclusively use part of your home for business, you can deduct a

- portion of rent/mortgage, utilities, and internet.
- Example: If your office is 10% of your home's square footage, you may deduct 10% of those costs.
- **Pro Tip:** If you own your home and take the deductions for the use of the home, you are also depreciating your home (the purchase price divided by 39 years). The depreciation taken for all the years that you have used the home office
- deduction will be recaptured when you sell your house and that will be taxed at the-then capital gains tax rate. Consult with your tax accountant on whether it is beneficial to claim the actual deductions of taking the Safe Harbor and deducting only the square footage (currently up to $1,500 and up to 300 square feet). If you are renting, it is beneficial to claim the home office deduction.
-

2. **Business Meals**
   - Meals with clients, prospects, or business partners are usually 50% deductible.
   - Temporary IRS rules (during certain tax years) allowed 100% for restaurant meals — check current guidelines.
   - Pro tip: Always jot down *who* you met and *what* you discussed. The IRS requires you to keep a log of the event: Who you took out to lunch/dinner; what was the purpose of the

- o meeting; what was discussed; cannot be anything extravagant.

3. Travel Expenses

When travel is **primarily for business**, the IRS lets you deduct a wide range of related costs.

- **Deductible**: Airfare, train tickets, Uber/Lyft, rental cars, gas, tolls, hotel stays, baggage fees, airport parking, even tips to bellhops or drivers.
- **Meals while traveling**: You can deduct 50% of business meals while away from your tax home.
- **Not deductible**: The personal/vacation portion of your trip.

Example:

- You fly to Chicago for a 3-day industry conference. Airfare, hotel, taxis, and meals during those 3 days = deductible.
- If you stay 2 extra days for sightseeing, those extra hotel nights and meals = not deductible.

Pro Tip: If 75% or more of the trip is for business, the entire airfare is deductible even if you mix in some vacation days.

4. Vehicle Expenses

If you use your car for business, you can deduct costs two ways:

1. **Standard Mileage Rate** – A per-mile deduction set annually by the IRS (e.g., 65.5¢ per mile in 2023).
   - o Covers gas, insurance, repairs, depreciation, etc.

       o   Simple and often generous if you drive a lot.
2. Actual Expense Method – Track and deduct your actual business percentage of gas, oil changes, insurance, lease payments, repairs, and depreciation.

Example:
- You drove 10,000 miles this year, 6,000 for business. Using standard mileage (65.5¢), you deduct $3,930.
- If you had high car expenses (e.g., luxury car or high repair costs), actual expense might be higher.

Must-do: **Keep a mileage log** (manual or with apps like MileIQ, Everlance). Without documentation, the IRS can disallow your deduction.

5. Professional Services
Almost all professional fees tied to your business are deductible:
- Accountant fees (tax prep, bookkeeping).
- Attorneys (contracts, trademarks, business formation).
- Business coaches or consultants.
- Payroll services.

Example: If you pay your accounting $2,500 for bookkeeping and tax filing, that's fully deductible.

Pro Tip: Even online freelance services (e.g., hiring a graphic designer on Upwork or Fiverr) fall under professional services.

6. Supplies & Equipment

- **Office supplies**: pens, paper, ink cartridges, postage, etc.
- **Equipment**: computers, printers, cameras, phones, monitors, software subscriptions.
- **Depreciation vs. Section 179**:
  - Normally, expensive items must be depreciated (deducted over several years).
  - But **Section 179** and **bonus depreciation** let many small businesses deduct the full cost upfront (e.g., buy a $2,000 computer → deduct $2,000 this year).

Example: You buy a new $1,200 laptop and a $500 printer. Both are deductible immediately under Section 179.

7. Insurance

Business-related insurance is generally deductible:

- General liability or professional liability.
- Malpractice insurance (for doctors, lawyers, consultants).
- Workers' comp if you have employees.
- Commercial auto insurance if you use a company vehicle.
- **Health insurance**: If you're self-employed and not eligible for an employer plan, you can often deduct your premiums (with limits).

Pro Tip: Life insurance premiums are not deductible unless the business is the direct beneficiary — which is rare.

8. Education & Training

If the training **improves your current business skills**, it's deductible:

- Online courses, workshops, certifications.
- Books, trade journals, or industry subscriptions.
- Conferences or seminars related to your field.

Example: A photographer buying a $300 online course on advanced editing = deductible.

Not deductible: A lawyer taking a real estate agent course to switch careers (that's "new trade" education).

9. Marketing & Advertising

Anything spent to promote your business counts:

- Digital ads (Google, Facebook, Instagram, LinkedIn).
- Print ads, flyers, brochures, direct mail.
- Business cards, logos, branding.
- Website design and hosting fees.
- Sponsorships (e.g., sponsoring a local charity run with your logo on the T-shirt).

Pro Tip: Meals with potential clients only count as a business meal (50% deductible), not advertising. Keep them separate.

10. Retirement Contributions

Small business owners can save on taxes and build wealth by contributing to retirement plans:

- **SEP IRA**: Easy to set up, allows contributions up to 25% of compensation (max $70,000 in 2025).

- **Solo 401(k)**: For self-employed with no employees (except spouse). Can contribute as both employer and employee, which means bigger limits.
- **SIMPLE IRA**: For businesses with fewer than 100 employees.

Example: If you made $80,000 in profit and contribute $20,000 to a Solo 401(k), you're only taxed on $60,000.

Pro Tip: Retirement plans are one of the most powerful legal ways to reduce your tax bill while keeping the money for your future.

Bottom Line: These deductions are not "loopholes" — they're intentional parts of the tax code designed to encourage business growth. The key is keeping receipts, maintaining logs, and separating personal from business spending.

The "Can't Write Off" Category (Common Myths & Mistakes)

Some things **feel** "business-y," but the IRS says nope. These are the expenses that trip up a lot of entrepreneurs — especially in their first few years.

1. **Personal Clothing**
   - A new Armani suit for client meetings? **Not deductible.** The IRS rule is simple: if the clothing is suitable for everyday wear, it's personal.
   - **Allowed:** Clothing that is *not suitable* outside of work (e.g., scrubs for a nurse, safety vests

- o for construction, branded uniforms, or T-shirts with your company logo).
- o **Not allowed:** That sleek Brooks Brothers blazer, even if you *only* wear it at work.

Rule of Thumb: If you could wear it to a wedding or a dinner party, it's not deductible.

2. **Commuting Costs**
   - o Driving from home to your **regular office** = personal commuting. Always nondeductible.
   - o Driving from your office to a client meeting, supplier, or conference = deductible mileage.

Pro Tip: If you work from a home office that qualifies as your "principal place of business," your drive from home to clients *can* count as business mileage. This is why many self-employed people benefit from establishing a legitimate home office.

3. **Fines & Penalties**
The IRS doesn't reward bad behavior.
   - o Parking tickets, speeding tickets, OSHA fines, IRS penalties, court-ordered payments = never deductible.
   - o Even if the expense occurred while "working," the government wants compliance, not reimbursement.

Example: You're late filing payroll taxes and pay a $500 penalty. That penalty stings twice — once to your wallet, and again because you can't deduct it.

4. **Personal Meals & Entertainment**
   o Grabbing dinner with your spouse = personal, unless your spouse is an actual employee and the meal has a bona fide business purpose.
   o Meals with clients or prospects = 50% deductible (if documented).
   o Entertainment (ball games, concerts, golf outings) was once partly deductible. Since 2018, **entertainment expenses are generally nondeductible** — unless it's directly tied to a business event (e.g., a catered seminar).

Example: Buying Yankees tickets for you and your client? Not deductible.
Example: Hosting a workshop at a rented space that includes refreshments? Deductible.

5. **Hobbies Disguised as Businesses**
If your "business" doesn't show a profit in at least 3 out of 5 years, the IRS may classify it as a **hobby.**
   o Hobby income is taxable, but hobby expenses aren't deductible against other income.

Example: Selling a few paintings a year doesn't make your art a "business" unless you're marketing, tracking expenses, and trying to earn a profit.

Gray Areas (Where People Get in Trouble)
These aren't outright forbidden, but they're often abused — and red-flagged in audits.

- **Cell Phone Bills**: Deduct only the business percentage. If 60% of calls are business, deduct 60%. Avoid writing off the whole bill unless it's a dedicated business line.
- **Family Members on Payroll**: Legit if they actually work (your 16-year-old runs your social media). Not legit if it's just a way to shift income.
- **Mixing Business & Personal Travel**: Fly to Orlando for a 2-day conference and stay 5 days for Disney? The airfare may be deductible (since the primary reason was business), but the extra hotel and park tickets aren't.

Rule of Thumb: Deduct only what directly relates to business.

The Audit-Proof Deduction Rule
Before you claim a deduction, ask yourself:
"If I had to explain this expense to an IRS auditor, would I feel comfortable?"
- If yes, and you have receipts → claim it.
- If no, or it feels like stretching → skip it.

Documentation is king:
- Keep receipts, invoices, or digital copies.
- Track mileage logs, appointment calendars, and notes.
- Retain records for at least **3 years** (some experts say **7** for big-ticket items or if you file late).

Real-World Example
- **Business Owner A**: Doesn't track expenses carefully. At year-end, they only deduct rent, payroll, and obvious bills. Tax bill = $12,000.
- **Business Owner B**: Tracks all legitimate deductions — home office, mileage, training, advertising, retirement contributions. Tax bill = $6,500.
- **Difference? $5,500 saved.** Same revenue, same profit — better records.

Bottom Line: Deductions aren't shady loopholes — they're deliberate incentives written into tax law. The danger comes from:
1. Trying to deduct personal expenses.
2. Slipping into gray areas without documentation.
3. Believing myths ("but my friend deducts their clothes!").

The winning formula:
Know what's real. Track it well. Keep your receipts. Sleep easy at night.

7. Avoiding Red Flags That Trigger Audits

The truth? Most IRS audits are **random.** You can do everything right and still get picked. But the IRS also uses **algorithms** (called the Discriminant Information Function, or DIF score) to flag returns that look unusual compared to others in the same industry and income level.

Here are the **most common red flags** that can increase your audit risk — and how to avoid them:

1. **Reporting Consistent Losses Year After Year**
- If your business shows losses **3 years in a row**, the IRS
  may decide you're not really running a business but a
  hobby (remember the hobby-loss rule).
- This is especially true in industries where people may mix
  passion with profit — photography, art, music, travel
  blogging.

How to Avoid It:
- Demonstrate a **profit motive** (marketing efforts, business
  plans, invoices, contracts).
- Show at least some years of profit. If you can't, document
  why (e.g., industry downturn, startup costs, pandemic
  disruption).

2. **Claiming Excessive Deductions Compared to
   Income**
- If your revenue is $60,000 but you claim $55,000 in
  deductions, the IRS will ask: *"How is this business surviving?"*
- The IRS compares your ratios to industry norms. For
  example, a consultant claiming 90% of income as
  expenses looks suspicious compared to the average
  consultant.

How to Avoid It:
- Be reasonable. Claim **only what's legitimate** and
  document it.
- If you do have unusually high deductions (say, a big
  equipment purchase), keep receipts and note the reason.

3. Not Reporting All Income

- The IRS gets copies of **1099s and W-2s** that you receive. If you "forget" to report one, their system automatically flags it.
- Even if you don't get a 1099 (e.g., smaller freelance jobs), the income is still taxable.

How to Avoid It:

- Keep a log of **all payments received** — checks, PayPal, Venmo, Zelle, cash.
- Reconcile your bank deposits with reported income.
- When in doubt, **report everything.** It's better to pay tax on a little extra than to trigger an audit.

4. Large Cash Transactions Without Documentation

- The IRS keeps a close eye on **cash-heavy businesses** (restaurants, salons, car washes, retail shops).
- Depositing or withdrawing more than **$10,000 in cash** in a single transaction triggers a **Currency Transaction Report (CTR)** to the IRS.
- Frequent smaller deposits (a.k.a. "structuring" to avoid the $10K rule) also raises suspicion.

How to Avoid It:

- Keep detailed **cash logs**.
- Deposit cash consistently, don't try to "game the system."
- Always issue receipts for cash sales.

5. Home Office Deduction Abuse

- The home office deduction is legitimate, but many abuse it (e.g., deducting their entire rent for a one-bedroom apartment).
- IRS auditors know this is a common overreach.

How to Avoid It:

- Deduct only the square footage used **exclusively and regularly** for business.
- Keep a floor plan or photos as proof.
- If audited, being able to point to a **separate desk/work area** can make all the difference.

6. Sudden, Unexplained Changes

- Revenue doubles but expenses stay the same?
- Or expenses double while revenue stays flat?
- Huge swings without explanation can invite questions.

How to Avoid It:

- Provide consistency year over year.
- If you do have a big change (major investment, hiring staff, launching new services), **document it** and be ready to explain.

7. Overly Generous Deductions in Certain Categories

The IRS pays close attention to deductions that are **frequently abused**:

- **Meals & Travel** → claiming every dinner out as a "business meeting."

- **Vehicle Expenses** → claiming 100% business use of a car (almost never realistic).
- **Charitable Donations** → claiming unusually high donations relative to income.

How to Avoid It:
- Use **logs** (mileage apps, receipts, notes on business purpose).
- Be honest about personal vs. business use.
- When donating, keep **official receipts** from charities.

8. Messy or Inconsistent Recordkeeping
- Missing receipts.
- Numbers that don't add up.
- Inconsistencies between your **business return and personal return** (e.g., your personal lifestyle doesn't match your reported income).

How to Avoid It:
- Use accounting software (QuickBooks, Xero, Wave).
- Save receipts digitally — apps like Expensify or Hubdoc make this easy.
- Have an accountant review your return if your situation is complex.

9. Golden Rule: Stay Clean, Be Consistent, Keep Proof
- **Stay Clean** → Don't stretch deductions into personal territory.
- **Be Consistent** → Report similar categories year to year. Sudden, dramatic changes should have a paper trail.

- **Keep Proof** → Receipts, logs, contracts, invoices. If you can **prove it**, you can deduct it confidently.

Bottom Line:
Audits are scary, but they don't have to be if you treat your business like a business. The IRS isn't out to get entrepreneurs — they just want fairness. If you avoid red flags, track your income and expenses properly, and keep documentation, you dramatically reduce your chances of ever facing an audit.

10. Working with a Tax Professional
Yes, you *can* file on your own — but most growing businesses benefit from an accountant, CPA, or tax advisor.

Running a business is already a full-time job. Add in payroll, invoicing, marketing, and customer service — and the last thing you want is to wrestle with the tax code at midnight in March. That's where a tax professional comes in.

Why Hire a Tax Professional?
1. **They Know the Law Better Than You**
   o The U.S. tax code is **thousands of pages** long and changes constantly. What was deductible last year might not be this year.
   o A good tax pro stays up to date on those changes so you don't miss deductions or accidentally break a rule.

2. **They Save You Money**
   - o Many business owners think, "I'll save money by doing my own taxes." In reality, the deductions you miss usually cost you more than a professional's fee.
   - o Example: A CPA or Enrolled Agent (explained later) might spot that you qualify for the **Qualified Business Income (QBI) deduction** or a **Section 179 deduction** you didn't know about — saving you thousands.

3. **They Save You Time**
   - o Every hour you spend figuring out tax forms is an hour you're not growing your business.
   - o Tax pros can complete in **hours** what might take you **days**.

4. **They Protect You in Case of Audit**
   - o If you're audited, you don't want to face the IRS alone.
   - o Many professionals will represent you or help prepare the documents you need to defend yourself.

Types of Tax Professionals

Not all tax preparers are the same. Here's the breakdown:

- **Certified Public Accountant (CPA):**
  - o Licensed, highly trained, can represent you before the IRS.
  - o Great for complex businesses, strategic tax planning, and long-term advice.
- **Enrolled Agent (EA):**
  - o Licensed directly by the IRS.

- Specialize in tax law and representation. Often less expensive than CPAs.
- **Tax Attorney:**
  - Best if you have legal trouble, tax disputes, or need help with complex business structures.
  - Usually more expensive, but essential for high-stakes cases.
- **Seasonal Tax Preparer (like chain services):**
  - Fine for simple individual returns.
  - Not ideal for businesses — they often lack deep knowledge of small business deductions.

Rule of Thumb: If you own a business, work with a seasoned accountant who provides all the services you need under one roof. That is the best way to take advantage of all that you and your business need.

How to Choose the Right Professional

1. **Industry Experience**
   - Pick someone who understands your type of business. An accountant who mainly works with restaurants may not be the best fit if you run an online coaching business.
2. **Ask About Their Credentials**
   - CPAs are licensed by the state. EAs are licensed by the IRS. Both are searchable online.
   - Don't just take their word for it — verify.

3. **Check Availability**
    o Some tax preparers disappear after April 15. You want someone available **year-round** for advice.
4. **Fee Structure**
    o Some charge hourly, others flat fees. Make sure you know what's included.
    o Be cautious of anyone who charges a percentage of your refund — that's a red flag.

When to Call in a Tax Pro

You don't always need a pro for everything, but here are signs you should:

- You had a major life change: started a business, hired employees, bought real estate, or got married/divorced.
- You're not sure which deductions apply.
- You're dealing with multiple states or international clients.
- You received an IRS letter or notice.
- You simply don't want the stress.

How to Work Effectively With a Tax Professional

Hiring a pro doesn't mean you can hand them a shoebox of receipts and disappear. You'll get better results if you:

- **Stay Organized:** Use accounting software, keep digital receipts, and reconcile your accounts monthly (or work with an accountant who provides those services to you).

- **Communicate:** Don't wait until April. Check in mid-year to see if you should adjust estimated taxes or take action before December 31.
- **Be Honest:** Hiding income or exaggerating expenses puts both you and your preparer at risk.

Real-World Example
- *Business Owner A* does their own taxes with software. They miss the home office depreciation and underpay estimated taxes. Cost: an IRS penalty plus $3,200 in missed deductions.
- *Business Owner B* hires an accountant who sets up a quarterly tax plan, maximizes deductions, and avoids penalties. Net savings: $4,500 — even after paying the accountant's fees.

Bottom Line: A good tax professional isn't an expense — it's an **investment.** They can save you money, time, and stress, while keeping you out of trouble. Think of them as part of your business team, just like a lawyer or a banker.

Quick Decision Guide
- If your business is **new, simple, and small**, starting with DIY software can work.
- Once you add employees, multiple income sources, or want to save aggressively on taxes, a **tax professional pays for themselves.**
- Rule of thumb: If you're spending more than **5 hours per year on taxes**, or losing sleep over it, it's time to hire help.

11. Taxes as a Strategic Tool

Most business owners think of taxes as a once-a-year burden — something to survive, not something to **leverage**. But the most successful entrepreneurs flip the script: they treat taxes as a **built-in strategy tool**. Instead of waiting until April to react, they use tax planning to guide decisions all year long.

Think of your tax return as a **report card** for how efficiently you're running your business. If you only look at it after the fact, you can't change your grade. But if you pay attention during the year, you can adjust your strategy and come out ahead.

Here's how taxes can become a strategic advantage:

Timing Income and Expenses

- If you know you'll have a higher profit year, you might **accelerate expenses** into December (buying equipment, prepaying rent, stocking supplies) to reduce taxable income now.
- If next year looks leaner, you might **delay income** by pushing invoices into January, balancing out the tax load.
- Pro tip: Always work with your tax professional to avoid cash-flow issues — tax savings aren't worth it if you run out of operating cash.

2. Choosing the Right Entity

- Your legal structure directly impacts taxes:
    - A sole proprietor pays **self-employment tax** on all profits.

- o An S-Corp can reduce those taxes through a "reasonable salary" + distributions strategy.
- o A C-Corp pays its own tax but can open unique deductions (like certain health benefits).
- Smart businesses review their structure **every few years** as revenue grows — what worked at $50K in revenue may be costing you thousands at $500K.

3. Leveraging Retirement Plans

- Contributions to a SEP IRA, SIMPLE IRA, or Solo 401(k) are deductible.
- Translation: you lower today's tax bill **and** build wealth for the future.
- Example: A self-employed consultant earning $120,000 can contribute up to $22,500 (2023 limit for Solo 401(k)) + 25% of net profit. That could save $15,000+ in taxes while setting up a nest egg.

4. Using Depreciation as a Cash-Flow Tool

- Equipment, vehicles, computers — normally these are deducted over several years.
- With **Section 179** and **bonus depreciation**, you can deduct most or all of the cost upfront.
- Smart owners use this strategically: buy when cash flow is strong, time deductions when you need them.
- Caution: Depreciation lowers today's taxes, but if you sell the asset later, **recapture rules** mean you

- may owe taxes back. A pro can help you balance the tradeoff.

5. Hiring Family Members
- If your kids legitimately work for your business, you can pay them wages, deduct the expense, and potentially move income into a lower tax bracket.
- Example: Paying your teenager $10,000 for real admin work means you deduct $10,000 from your business income. If they're under the standard deduction threshold, they may pay **zero tax** on it.
- Win-win: lower business tax + family wealth building.

6. Turning Benefits into Deductions
- Health insurance premiums (in many cases), retirement contributions, professional development, and even a portion of your cell phone and internet bills can be structured as deductible expenses.
- The more you can shift personal spending into legitimate business deductions, the less taxable income you have.

7. State & Local Incentives
- Many states and cities offer tax credits for:
  - Hiring employees in targeted areas
  - Investing in green technology
  - Training and workforce development
- Most small businesses never claim them because they don't know they exist. A little research can uncover thousands in savings.

8. Taxes as a Decision-Making Filter

- Considering buying or leasing equipment? Taxes can tip the scales.
- Unsure about expanding into a new state? Sales tax and state income tax laws should be part of your research.
- Thinking of selling your business? Structuring the deal as an asset sale vs. stock sale can mean **millions in difference** in tax liability.

Bottom Line: Taxes are not just about compliance — they're a **financial steering wheel**. Every dollar you save in taxes is a dollar you can reinvest in marketing, hiring, or growth. The difference between businesses that "get by" and those that **scale** often comes down to using the tax code proactively instead of reactively.

12. The Big Picture

When you step back from all the details — deductions, forms, quarterly payments, strategies — it's easy to lose sight of why taxes matter in the first place. Taxes aren't just numbers on a return.

They're a reflection of your **business decisions, financial health, and growth trajectory.**
Think of it like this:

- **Your sales** show how well you're attracting customers.
- **Your expenses** show how well you're managing resources.
- **Your tax return** shows how well you've translated those two into *real wealth*.

Taxes sit at the crossroads of compliance and opportunity. Play them passively, and you're at the mercy of the IRS bill every April. Play them strategically, and you can turn the tax code into a **profit partner**.

1. Taxes Reflect the Story of Your Business

Every line on your tax return tells part of your story:

- High travel and meals might mean you're aggressively growing your network.
- Big equipment purchases signal reinvestment.
- Retirement contributions reflect forward thinking. Instead of dreading your return, see it as a **mirror** of how you've built (or failed to build) habits that align with growth.

2. Taxes Are Not an Annual Event

Too many entrepreneurs treat taxes like a **fire drill**: pile up receipts, dump them on an accountant, hope for the best. The truth? Taxes are an **everyday business activity**.

- Every time you choose how to pay yourself.
- Every time you decide to lease or buy.
- Every time you log miles or skip logging them.

These micro-decisions ripple into thousands of dollars saved or lost at year-end.

3. A Balanced Mindset: Save, But Don't Starve Growth

Some business owners obsess over deductions, squeezing every penny, but never step back to ask: *"Am I cutting myself off from growth?"*

- Example: You could avoid taxes by never showing profit — but no lender or investor will take you seriously.
- On the flip side, ignoring deductions is like burning money.
  The goal is balance: **optimize taxes without strangling growth.**

4. Plan Beyond the Current Year

Smart tax planning is about the **long game**:

- Reducing taxable income today is great — unless it hurts you in two years when you want a loan and show zero profit.
- Shifting income into retirement accounts lowers today's tax bill, but also sets you up for **wealth compounding** decades down the line.
- Structuring your business today (LLC, S-Corp, C-Corp) affects not just April 15th but also how you exit the business, sell it, or pass it on.

5. Taxes and Peace of Mind

There's also a psychological payoff. Nothing creates stress like unexpected tax bills. Nothing creates confidence like knowing:

- You've set aside money for quarterly taxes.
- You understand your deductions.
- You're not living in fear of an audit.
  When taxes are handled with foresight, they stop being a source of anxiety and become part of your **business rhythm.**

6. Taxes as a Wealth-Building Lever

For high earners especially, taxes are often the **largest expense**. By managing them intentionally:

- You free up capital for marketing campaigns.
- You keep more money to invest in real estate, retirement, or expansion.
- You shorten the time it takes to build true financial independence.

Put simply: every dollar saved in taxes is a dollar that can **work for you instead of the IRS**.

Bottom Line: The big picture of taxes isn't about loopholes or fear. It's about understanding that the tax system is built to reward business activity — investment, hiring, innovation, retirement saving. If you align your business decisions with those incentives, you not only cut your tax bill but also accelerate your growth.

Taxes aren't the enemy — they're a **compass**. And when you learn to read it, you can steer your business with far more clarity and confidence.

Chapter 8 – Avoiding Common Small Business Accounting Mistakes

Running a business is hard enough without letting preventable accounting mistakes eat away at your profits, stress levels, and time. The truth is, most small business owners don't fail because they couldn't sell — they fail because they lost track of the numbers.

Accounting mistakes don't just cost money; they cost **clarity**. And when you don't have clarity, you can't make good decisions. The good news? Most mistakes are completely avoidable with the right systems and habits.

Mixing Business and Personal Finances

The Mistake

Many entrepreneurs start their business using their personal bank account because it feels simpler — why open a new account when you already have one? Before long, you're paying the electric bill and client lunch out of the same debit card. When tax season rolls around, you're stuck combing through hundreds of transactions, trying to remember what was "personal" and what was "business."

Examples of this mistake include:

- **Using one bank account for everything**: groceries, rent, office supplies, and client invoices all flowing in and out together.
- **Paying the electric bill and business expenses with the same debit card**, without documenting which is which.

- **Guessing at year-end**: "Hmm, was that $427 Amazon order office supplies… or a new TV for my living room?"

It may seem harmless at first, but it's one of the fastest ways to create accounting chaos.

Why It Hurts

Mixing finances doesn't just make things messy — it creates serious risks:

- **Recordkeeping nightmare:** You'll spend hours separating transactions manually, often incorrectly. This leads to sloppy books, higher bookkeeping and accounting costs, and potential tax mistakes.
- **Missed deductions:** If you can't clearly prove an expense was business-related, you'll lose the deduction. You'll pay higher taxes. That's money left on the table.
- **Legal liability:** If you're ever audited, sued, or need to defend your business, blurred finances make it harder to argue that your business is separate from your personal assets. In extreme cases, it can lead to "piercing the corporate veil," where your personal property (like your house or car) is at risk.

Think of it this way: if your personal and business finances are tangled together, the IRS, your bank, or a lawyer will assume **your business isn't really separate from you.** That's the opposite of what you want.

The Fix

The good news is that fixing this problem is straightforward:

1. **Open a separate business checking account** — even if you're a sole proprietor. Having a dedicated account is like drawing a bright line between "you" and "your business."

2. **Use a dedicated business debit or credit card.** That way, every swipe is automatically a business expense. No second-guessing later.

3. **Pay yourself properly.** Instead of using the company card for groceries, transfer money from your business account to your personal account as either:
   - A **salary** (if you're on payroll), or
   - An **owner's draw** (if you're self-employed). This makes it crystal clear what is "personal income" vs. "business expense."

Pro Tip: If you occasionally need to pay for a business expense with a personal card (it happens!), reimburse yourself right away. Write a note in your records, and transfer the exact amount from the business account back to your personal account.

Bottom Line:

Mixing business and personal finances is the #1 rookie mistake — but also one of the easiest to fix. Once your accounts are separate, every transaction tells a clear story, your tax prep is smoother, and your liability protection is stronger.

Neglecting to Reconcile Accounts

The Mistake

Many small business owners rely on their bank account as their "accounting system." If the balance looks healthy, they assume everything's fine. They may never open their monthly bank or credit card statements, or they glance quickly without comparing them to their books.

At first glance, this seems harmless — after all, the bank shows you what's really there, right? But this shortcut skips an essential step: **reconciliation** — the process of matching your internal accounting records with what the bank (or credit card company) says actually happened.

Why It Hurts

Skipping reconciliation creates a silent snowball effect:

- **Small errors compound into big ones.**
  A $50 double charge or a missing deposit may not seem like much, but over 12 months, those errors pile up. Suddenly your books don't match reality.
- **Fraud and mistakes slip by.**
  Without reconciliation, you might miss unauthorized charges, fraudulent transactions, or even bank errors. (Yes, banks make mistakes too!)
- **Unreliable financial reports.**
  If your accounts aren't reconciled, your Profit & Loss and Balance Sheet may be completely wrong. That means your tax return is wrong, your loan applications are wrong, and your decision-making is based on bad data.

- **IRS red flags.**

  Inconsistent or inaccurate records increase your risk in an audit. If the IRS finds mismatches between what you reported and what hit your bank, it's a problem.

Think of reconciliation as the "trust but verify" step of accounting. Just because money shows in your account doesn't mean your books captured it correctly.

The Fix

The solution is simple — and surprisingly quick when done regularly:

1. **Reconcile monthly.**

   At the end of each month, compare your accounting records (QuickBooks, Xero, or even a manual ledger) to your bank and credit card statements.

2. **Look for differences.**

   If the bank shows a $500 check cleared but your books don't, fix it. If your books show a $200 deposit but the bank doesn't, investigate.

3. **Leverage your software.**

   Modern tools like QuickBooks, Xero, or Wave let you link your bank account directly. With automation, reconciliation becomes a quick task instead of a dreaded project.

4. **Make it a habit.**

   Put reconciliation on your end-of-month checklist (see Chapter 6). If you stay on top of it, it's painless. Skip three or four months, and it becomes overwhelming.

Real-World Example

A local café owner relied only on their online bank balance. Their point-of-sale system had a glitch that duplicated some credit card deposits in their books. For months, their books showed more income than the bank actually deposited. When tax season came, they almost overpaid by thousands in taxes — because their "profit" was inflated by errors. A simple monthly reconciliation would have caught it quickly.

Bottom Line:

Reconciliation isn't busywork — it's the safeguard that keeps your books accurate, your reports reliable, and your business protected from both mistakes and fraud.

Poor Recordkeeping of Expenses

The Mistake

Many small business owners fall into the "shoebox method" of accounting: throwing receipts into a box, envelope, or glove compartment — promising themselves they'll sort it out "at tax time."

Other common slip-ups include:

- **Not tracking mileage, tips, or small cash purchases.** Those $8 parking fees and $20 lunches feel trivial, but they add up to hundreds (or even thousands) by year-end.
- **Forgetting what purchases were for.** Six months later, you may not remember whether that $427 Amazon order was for printer toner (deductible) or patio furniture (personal).

- **Mixing personal with business.** Buying business supplies with your personal credit card and never logging it.

It feels harmless in the moment, but this disorganization creates big problems down the line.

Why It Hurts
Poor recordkeeping has real costs:
- **Lost deductions.** If you can't prove an expense, you usually can't deduct it. That's money left on the table.
- **Stressful audits.** The IRS doesn't accept "I think this was business-related" as evidence. If you don't have receipts, logs, or invoices, deductions can be denied.
- **Wasted time.** Sorting a year's worth of receipts under deadline is overwhelming. You'll miss items just to get it done.
- **Inaccurate financials.** Without proper categorization, you can't see where your money is going — which makes it harder to cut costs or forecast cash flow.

Think of it this way: **your records are the receipts that "buy" your deductions. Without them, you're overpaying taxes.**

The Fix
Fortunately, technology has made expense tracking almost painless:
1. **Use a receipt-tracking app.**
   Tools like **Expensify, Hubdoc, or even QuickBooks mobile** let you snap a photo of a

2. receipt and categorize it on the spot. Many apps automatically read the date, amount, and vendor.

3. **Track mileage with apps.**

   IRS requires a mileage log if you deduct car expenses. Apps like **MileIQ** or **Everlance** run in the background, tracking every trip and letting you swipe left for personal, right for business.

4. **Categorize in real time.**

   Don't wait until December. Set aside 5 minutes a week to review and tag expenses. Doing it as you go keeps details fresh in your mind.

5. **Keep records long enough.**

   The IRS recommends at least **3 years**, but many tax pros suggest **7 years** for peace of mind. Cloud storage (Google Drive, Dropbox, OneDrive) makes this easy.

6. **Link your bank and credit cards.**

   Most accounting software automatically pulls in

7. transactions, making reconciliation (see Section 2) faster and more accurate.

Real-World Example

A freelance designer used to toss all receipts into a shoebox. At tax time, she spent three stressful days sorting crumpled paper, only to realize she had lost receipts for multiple Uber rides, client meals, and a new laptop. Without proof, her accountant couldn't claim them. Estimated loss: **over $2,000 in missed deductions**. The next year, she switched to an app that synced with her credit card. Every transaction popped up on her phone, where she snapped a receipt photo and added a quick note. When tax season came, her accountant had a clean digital folder and saved her thousands.

Bottom Line:

Good records are money in the bank. Every receipt, every mile, every small expense matters. With modern tools, there's no excuse for the shoebox method anymore.

Misclassifying Workers (Employee vs. Contractor)

The Mistake

Business owners sometimes think they've hacked the system:

- "If I just pay them as a contractor, I don't have to deal with payroll, benefits, or taxes."
- On paper, it seems cheaper and easier.

But if you **treat someone like an employee**, the IRS (and often state labor agencies) will classify them as one — no matter what their title or what your contract says.

Common slip-ups:

- A "contractor" who works 40 hours per week, only for your company.
- Requiring them to follow your office schedule and company handbook.
- Providing all the equipment, software, and workspace.
- Paying them a steady weekly or monthly amount instead of per project.

Why It Hurts

1. **IRS Penalties & Back Taxes**

   If the IRS reclassifies a contractor as an employee, you may owe:

   o Payroll taxes (Social Security, Medicare, unemployment).

   o Back withholdings for income tax.

     o   Penalties and interest — sometimes years' worth.

2. **Labor Law Exposure**

Workers may claim:

     o   Overtime they should have been paid.

     o   Benefits like vacation, retirement contributions, and health insurance.

     o   Wrongful termination protection.

3. **State-Level Scrutiny**

States like California (AB5 law) and Massachusetts use the **ABC test**, which is stricter than the federal IRS test.

     o   In some states, almost everyone is considered an employee unless you can prove otherwise.

4. **Reputation Risk**

Getting caught misclassifying workers damages trust — with employees, clients, and regulators.

The Fix

1. **Know the IRS Tests**

The IRS uses three categories:

     o   **Behavioral Control** – Do you decide when, where, and how they work?

     o   **Financial Control** – Do you control pay structure, reimburse expenses, or prevent profit/loss?

     o   **Relationship** – Do you offer benefits, expect a long-term relationship, or label them "staff"?

If you control the *what* and *how*, they're an employee.

2. **Use Strong Contracts for Contractors**

- o Define the project scope, timeline, and payment terms.
- o State clearly they set their own hours and methods.
- o Require them to use their own tools/software when possible.
- o Allow them to work for multiple clients.

3. **Classify Conservatively**
   - o If you're unsure, classify as an employee — it's safer and often cheaper in the long run.
   - o Payroll software (Gusto, ADP, QuickBooks Payroll) automates compliance and filings.

4. **Limit Contractor Engagements**
   - o Keep them project-based, not ongoing roles.
   - o Avoid calling them "team members" or giving them employee perks.

Gray Areas Where Owners Get in Trouble

- **Family Members on Payroll**
  - o Legitimate if your spouse or kids actually *work* in the business. They must perform real duties, track hours, and get reasonable pay.
  - o Fake "jobs" (paying your child $10,000 for "helping with the website" when they didn't) can trigger audits.

Pro Tip: Keep timesheets, assign real tasks, and pay fair market wages.

- **Interns**
  - o If an intern provides work that benefits your company, they usually must be classified (and

- o paid) as an **employee** under the Fair Labor
  Standards Act (FLSA).
- o Unpaid internships are legal only in narrow cases
  (e.g., primarily educational, student receives more
  benefit than the company).

Pro Tip: When in doubt, pay them at least minimum wage.

- **Gig Workers / Freelancers**
  - o Platforms like Upwork or Fiverr make hiring
    contractors easy. But remember:
  - o If they're working full-time only for you, they're
    more like employees.
  - o If they're juggling multiple clients and projects,
    they're safely contractors.

Pro Tip: Don't blur the lines. Keep gigs project-based.

- **On-Call or "Perma-Temps"**
  - o Hiring a "contractor" for two years in the same
    seat as an employee is a red flag.
  - o Long-term exclusivity looks like employment, not
    contracting.

The Audit-Proof Rule of Thumb

Ask yourself:
"If I had to explain this worker's role to an IRS auditor, would I
feel 100% confident they meet the definition of
contractor/employee?"

If you hesitate, reclassify.

Real-World Example

- **Bad Case:** A design firm called its full-time graphic artist a "contractor." He worked in-office, 9–5, using company software. After an audit, the IRS demanded $45,000 in back payroll taxes and penalties. The artist also filed a claim for overtime.

- **Good Case:** Another firm hired a freelance illustrator on a per-project basis. She set her own schedule, worked from her own studio, and had 5 other clients. Even after review, her classification stood as a legitimate contractor.

Bottom Line:

Misclassifying workers isn't a harmless shortcut — it's one of the fastest ways to rack up tax debt and legal trouble. Protect yourself with the right classifications, contracts, and documentation. When in doubt, err on the side of caution.

Forgetting Sales Tax (If Applicable)

The Mistake

Sales tax rules vary wildly from state to state (and sometimes even city to city). But many business owners make dangerous assumptions, like:

- **Collecting sales tax but not remitting it** — treating it as part of business revenue and spending it.
- **Not collecting sales tax at all** because they didn't realize they were required to.
- **Assuming digital goods or services aren't taxable** when, in many states, they are.

- **Expanding into other states online** and ignoring *nexus* rules (economic thresholds that require you to collect tax in those states).

Why It Hurts

1. **It's Not Your Money**
   - States treat sales tax as **trust money** — you're essentially holding it on behalf of the government.
   - Spending it is like "borrowing" from the state, and they don't take kindly to it.

2. **Severe Penalties**
   - Interest and late fees add up quickly.
   - In some jurisdictions, failing to remit sales tax is considered **theft** and can carry **criminal charges**.

3. **Audit Magnet**
   - States conduct regular **sales tax audits** because it's easy revenue.
   - A small bookkeeping mistake (forgetting to remit tax on a single product line) can snowball into years of back taxes and penalties.

4. **Online Sales Expansion**
   - After the *South Dakota v. Wayfair (2018)* Supreme Court ruling, states can require businesses to collect sales tax even without physical presence
   - — simply crossing a revenue or transaction threshold can create "economic nexus."

o   Example: Make 200 sales into New York from another state? You might owe sales tax there.

The Fix

1.   **Register with Your State Tax Authority**
     o   If your products or services are taxable, apply for a sales tax permit.
     o   Never start collecting sales tax without being registered — in many states, that's illegal.

2.   **Separate the Money**
     o   Open a dedicated account for sales tax.
     o   Each time you collect, transfer the tax portion into that account immediately. That way, you never risk "accidentally" spending it.

3.   **Automate Tracking & Filing**
     o   Most modern **POS systems** (Square, Shopify, Clover) and **accounting software** (QuickBooks, Xero) can automatically:
         ▪   Calculate the right tax based on location.
         ▪   Track amounts collected.
         ▪   Prepare remittance reports.
     o   Many states also allow e-filing and auto-payments

4.   **Stay on Top of Nexus Rules**
     o   If you sell online, regularly review whether you've crossed thresholds in other states.
     o   Tools like **Avalara** or **TaxJar** can monitor nexus across states and simplify compliance.

5.   **Know What's Taxable in Your State**
     o   Tangible products almost always are.

- o Services, digital goods, SaaS subscriptions, and labor charges vary state by state.
- o Don't assume — check your state's Department of Revenue guidance.

Gray Areas to Watch Out For

- **Shipping & Handling Fees** – Sometimes taxable, sometimes not.
- **Coupons & Discounts** – Sales tax may apply to the *pre-discount* amount in some states.
- **Digital Goods** – Music downloads, e-books, and even online courses may be taxable depending on the jurisdiction.
- **Marketplace Sales** – Platforms like Amazon or Etsy may handle sales tax for you, but not always for every state. Double-check.

Real-World Example
- **The Costly Mistake:** A boutique shop collected sales tax faithfully but kept it in their general operating account.
- When cash ran short, they dipped into the tax funds to cover payroll. By the time the state audited, they owed **$25,000 in unremitted taxes, plus interest and penalties.**
- **The Smart Fix:** Another retailer linked their POS directly to a "sales tax savings" account. Each night, the system automatically transferred tax collected into that account. When filing time came, the money was waiting — stress-free.

Bottom Line:
Sales tax isn't optional, and it isn't your money. Treat it like you're safeguarding government funds, separate it from operations, and lean on automation to stay compliant — especially if you sell online.

Not Tracking Accounts Receivable (A/R) Properly

The Mistake
It's one of the most common small business blind spots:

- **Sending invoices but not following up.** You assume clients will pay on time, but weeks go by with silence.
- **Forgetting unpaid invoices** until cash flow suddenly dries up.
- **Mixing "open" and "closed" invoices** in your system — you think you've been paid when you haven't.
- **No formal collections process.** Each overdue invoice is handled differently, if at all.

Why It Hurts
1. **Revenue on Paper ≠ Cash in the Bank**
   - An invoice is not cash. You can't pay employees or rent with "accounts receivable."
   - Too many unpaid invoices create a false sense of security in your financial reports.
2. **Cash Flow Crunch**
   - Late payments from clients can leave you scrambling to cover payroll, rent, or vendor bills.

- o Businesses don't fail because of lack of sales —
  they fail because of lack of cash.

3. **Strained Client Relationships**
   - o Inconsistent or overly aggressive collections
     damage trust.
   - o Clients may "forget" you if you don't remind
     them — but they may also resent surprise
     collections actions.

4. **Snowball Effect**
   - o The longer an invoice goes unpaid, the less likely
     it is you'll collect it.
   - o By 90 days overdue, industry studies show
     collection chances drop to **less than 50%.**

The Fix

1. **Run A/R Aging Reports Monthly (Minimum)**
   - o Break invoices into "Current, 30, 60, 90+ days
     past due."
   - o This immediately shows you where trouble is
     brewing.

2. **Follow a Clear Collection System**
   - o **Day 15:** Send a **friendly reminder** (assume they
     just forgot).
   - o **Day 30:** Send a **firm reminder** with the updated
     balance and due date.
   - o **Day 60+:** Consider adding **late fees or interest**
     (if in your contracts) or escalate to collections.
   - o Consistency matters more than aggression.

3. **Automate the Process**
   - o Most accounting systems (QuickBooks,
     FreshBooks, Xero) can automatically:

- Email reminders.
- Apply late fees.
- Generate aging reports.
  - Set it up once, and the system chases payments for you.
4. **Incentivize Early Payments**
   - Offer discounts like **"2% off if paid in 10 days."**
   - This can speed up cash flow without damaging margins.
5. **Set Clear Terms Upfront**
   - Define payment terms in your contracts (Net 15, Net 30, etc.).
   - Make sure invoices clearly state due dates, penalties, and acceptable payment methods.
6. **Make Paying Easy**
   - Accept ACH, credit cards, or online payments.
   - The easier you make it, the faster you get paid.

Gray Areas to Watch Out For

- **Large Clients:** Sometimes the biggest clients take the longest to pay — don't be afraid to hold them accountable.
- **Cash vs. Accrual Accounting:** Under accrual, revenue shows when invoiced, not when collected. Without close A/R monitoring, your books can look healthier than your bank account.
- **Partial Payments:** Always document them clearly. Partial payments can create confusion if not tracked correctly.

Real-World Example

- **The Costly Mistake:** A marketing agency had $120,000 in outstanding invoices but thought business was booming. When rent came due, they discovered less than $10,000 in the bank. They had to max out credit cards to cover payroll.
- **The Smart Fix:** Another agency ran **weekly A/R aging reports**. They spotted a client trending late at 30 days and called immediately. The client admitted they had cash flow issues but arranged a payment plan. The agency avoided a bigger crisis by catching it early.

Bottom Line:

Invoices are promises, not payments. If you're not monitoring accounts receivable like a hawk, you're not really managing your cash flow. Make it a system, automate reminders, and never assume money is coming in until it's in your bank.

Ignoring Payroll Compliance

The Mistake

Payroll seems simple — pay your employees and move on. But it's one of the most **regulated and scrutinized areas** of running a business. Common mistakes include:

- **Paying employees "under the table."** Skipping payroll taxes by handing out cash.
- **Missing payroll tax deadlines.** Forgetting to file quarterly reports or remit withheld taxes.

- **Miscalculating overtime, benefits, or PTO.** Especially in industries with hourly staff, irregular shifts, or tipped workers.
- **Misclassifying workers.** Calling someone a contractor when they're really an employee.
- **Not documenting properly.** Lacking timesheets, signed pay stubs, or benefits records.

Why It Hurts

1. **IRS Trouble**
   - Payroll taxes are the **#1 compliance area** where small businesses get into trouble.
   - If you withhold taxes from employees and don't remit them, the IRS considers it **theft** — penalties are severe and personal liability often applies.

2. **Massive Penalties**
   - Missing payroll deadlines can trigger fines, penalties, and interest that quickly snowball.
   - Even small errors (like misreporting Social Security withholdings) can lead to audits.

3. **Employee Trust**
   - Employees count on accurate, timely paychecks.
   - If checks are late, benefits mishandled, or overtime miscalculated, **morale drops fast.**
   - Payroll mistakes can push employees to leave and damage your reputation as an employer.

4. **Legal Risks**
   - Wage/hour laws are strict, especially around overtime, minimum wage, and benefits.

- o Violations can lead to lawsuits, Department of Labor investigations, and class actions.

The Fix

1. **Use Payroll Software or Services**
   - o Your payroll service provider handles:
     - ▪ Tax withholdings automatically.
     - ▪ Direct deposits.
     - ▪ Year-end W-2 and 1099 filings.
   - o Outsourcing payroll often costs less than fixing compliance mistakes.

2. **File Reports on Time**
   - o Federal: Form 941 (quarterly), Form 940 (annual FUTA), W-2/W-3 at year-end.
   - o State: Withholding returns and unemployment tax reports (varies by state).
   - o Missing these deadlines is the fastest way to attract penalties.

3. **Stay Updated on Wage/Hour Laws**
   - o Minimum wage laws differ by state (and sometimes by city).
   - o Overtime rules (time-and-a-half after 40 hours/week federally, but some states require daily overtime).
   - o New rules pop up frequently (e.g., exempt vs. non-exempt salary thresholds).

4. **Document Everything**
   - o Timesheets (manual or digital).
   - o Signed employee agreements.
   - o Payroll registers and pay stubs.
   - o Proper recordkeeping is your first defense if audited.

5. **Avoid "Under the Table" Payroll**
   o Paying cash may feel easier but creates **huge liability.**
   o If discovered, you'll owe back taxes, penalties, and possibly face fraud charges.

Gray Areas to Watch Out For

- **Tipped Employees:** Tracking tips accurately for tax purposes.
- **Remote Workers:** Tax obligations may apply in multiple states.
- **Bonuses & Fringe Benefits:** These must be reported as taxable income unless specifically excluded.

Real-World Example

- **The Costly Mistake:** A restaurant paid servers in cash to avoid payroll taxes. When the IRS audited, the owner was hit with **back taxes, penalties, and interest exceeding $150,000.** The business nearly closed.
- **The Smart Fix:** Another small business switched to a payroll provider (Gusto). Payroll taxes were automatically filed, reports generated, and compliance headaches eliminated. The owner said it was the **"best money I spend each month."**

Bottom Line: Payroll is not a place to cut corners. The IRS and state agencies take it seriously, and employees depend on it. Get help, automate where you can, and never "wing it" when it comes to paying people.

Overreliance on Spreadsheets

The Mistake

Spreadsheets are a great tool — but they're not a full accounting system. Many small businesses make the mistake of using Excel (or Google Sheets) as their **only source of financial truth**:

- **Running the entire business in Excel.** Income, expenses, payroll, invoices — all manually entered.
- **No checks or balances.** No built-in controls to catch mistakes or enforce consistency.
- **Formula errors that go unnoticed.** A single misplaced decimal or broken cell reference can quietly skew results.
- **No audit trail.** Anyone can change numbers without leaving a record of what was changed and when.

Why It Hurts

1. **One Mistake Can Snowball**
   - A single typo or deleted row can ripple through your formulas and throw off months of financial data.
   - Many businesses have filed taxes or made big financial decisions based on incorrect spreadsheet numbers.

2. **Spreadsheets Don't Scale**
   - Fine when you're solo with a handful of transactions a month.
   - Once you hire staff, open a second location, or start dealing with inventory, spreadsheets collapse under the weight of complexity.

3. **No Built-In Compliance**
   - Spreadsheets don't generate IRS-ready reports (P&L, Balance Sheet, Cash Flow).
   - No built-in payroll tax filings, sales tax tracking, or depreciation schedules.
4. **Data Security Risks**
   - Spreadsheets are often emailed around — meaning multiple versions exist with no central source of truth.
   - Easy to lose or overwrite. If your laptop dies without a backup, years of records could vanish.

The Fix
1. **Transition to Accounting Software Early**
   - Cloud platforms like **QuickBooks Online, Xero, or Wave** are designed to handle business finances with accuracy and compliance in mind.
   - They automate journal entries, reconciliations, and tax-ready reporting.
2. **Use Spreadsheets for Analysis — Not as the System of Record**
   - Keep your **"source of truth"** in accounting software.
   - Use spreadsheets for:
     - Budget forecasting.
     - What-if scenarios.
     - Custom reports or visualizations.
3. **Build a Habit of Automation**
   - Import bank feeds automatically into software.

o Set up recurring invoices and payment reminders.
o The less you manually key in, the fewer mistakes you'll make.

Gray Areas to Watch Out For

- **Hybrid Systems:** Many businesses start with accounting software but keep running shadow spreadsheets on the side. This creates duplicate work and confusion about which numbers are "real."
- **Spreadsheet Overconfidence:** Just because you're good with Excel formulas doesn't mean it's the safest or most efficient choice for official financial data.

Real-World Example

- **The Risky Path:** A marketing agency tracked all revenue and expenses in Google Sheets. One copy-paste error inflated expenses by $30,000. They underpaid taxes for the year and faced penalties.
- **The Smarter Path:** Another agency invested in QuickBooks early. While they still used Excel for budgeting and campaign cost analysis, their **official books** were
- handled by the software, ensuring accuracy and compliance.

Bottom Line: Spreadsheets are a powerful sidekick — but a terrible accountant. Use them for insights, not as your main accounting system.

Not Reviewing Financial Reports

The Mistake (What actually happens)

- **Bank-balance management:** Decisions are made because "there's money in the account," not because the business is profitable or solvent.
- **Reports go unread:** The **P&L**, **Balance Sheet**, and **Cash Flow Statement** exist in your software but aren't opened, or they're skimmed without context.
- **No comparisons:** Numbers aren't compared to **last month, last year,** or **budget/forecast,** so trends are invisible.

Why It Hurts (What you don't see will hurt you)

- **Trends go unnoticed:** Declining **gross margin %,** creeping **overhead,** or rising **refund rates** continue for months before anyone acts.
- **Cash surprises:** Profitable companies can still run out of cash because receivables ballooned, inventory piled up, or debt service increased.
- **Missed upside:** You don't spot high-margin products, loyal cohorts, or channels with stellar ROAS because you're not segmenting the numbers.

The Fix (Make reports a decision ritual)
A. Read the "big three" with purpose
1. **Profit & Loss (P&L)** — performance over a period
   o **What to scan first:**
      ▪ **Revenue by line** (product/service) — growing? seasonal?
      ▪ **Gross margin %** = (Revenue − COGS) ÷ Revenue. Is it improving or slipping?

- **Operating expense ratio** = Opex ÷ Revenue. Is overhead scaling with growth?
- **Net margin** = Net Income ÷ Revenue. Are we keeping what we sell?

  o **Questions to ask:**
  - Which 3 expense lines rose fastest vs. last month/last year? Why?
  - Did price changes or discounting move gross margin?

2. **Balance Sheet** — snapshot of health
   o **What to scan first:**
   - **Cash, A/R, Inventory, A/P, Debt, Owner's Equity.**
   - **Liquidity:**
     - **Current ratio** = Current Assets ÷ Current Liabilities (comfort often ≥1.2, industry-dependent).
     - **Quick ratio** = (Cash + A/R) ÷ Current Liabilities (inventory excluded).

   o **Questions to ask:**
   - Is A/R growing faster than sales (collection problem)?
   - Is inventory rising with flat sales (overbuying, obsolete stock)?
   - Any short-term liabilities coming due next 90 days?

3. **Cash Flow Statement** — where cash actually moved
   o **Operating cash flow:** Are core operations generating cash?
   o **Investing cash flow:** Big asset buys? (vehicles, equipment)
   o **Financing cash flow:** New debt, repayments, owner draws/distributions.
   o **Questions to ask:**
      - Profitable but negative operating cash— what drove it (A/R, inventory, prepaids)?
      - Do we have **runway** (cash ÷ average monthly burn) of at least 2–3 months?

B. Build a monthly 60-minute review cadence
Before the meeting (done by bookkeeper):
- Close & **reconcile** all accounts.
- Tag/categorize properly; post accruals if you use accrual basis.

During the meeting (owner + finance lead):
1. **10 min — Flash checks:** Cash today vs. last month; any red alerts (tax due, payroll, covenants).
2. **20 min — P&L deep dive:** Revenue by line, gross margin %, top 5 expense movers, variance to budget.
3. **15 min — Balance Sheet health:** A/R aging, inventory days, A/P timing, current/quick ratios.
4. **10 min — Cash:** 13-week cash forecast update; upcoming large outflows/inflows.
5. **5 min — Actions:** Assign 3–5 concrete actions with owners & due dates.

Pro Tip: Save a standard report pack in your software: **P&L by Month (12 months), P&L vs Budget, Balance Sheet (current & prior), Cash Flow (YTD), A/R Aging, A/P Aging.**

C. Use the right KPIs (keep it small and sharp)
Core financial KPIs (most businesses):

- **Gross margin %** = (Revenue − COGS) ÷ Revenue.
- **Net margin %** = Net Income ÷ Revenue.
- **Operating expense ratio** = Opex ÷ Revenue
- **DSO (Days Sales Outstanding)** ≈ (A/R ÷ Avg Daily Sales). Lower = faster cash.
- **DPO (Days Payable Outstanding)** ≈ (A/P ÷ Avg Daily COGS). Not too high (supplier strain) or too low (cash left on table).
- **DIO (Days Inventory Outstanding)** ≈ (Inventory ÷ Avg Daily COGS). Lower = leaner stock.
- **Cash Conversion Cycle (CCC)** = DIO + DSO − DPO. Shorter = better.

Service businesses:

- **Utilization rate, effective hourly rate, churn/retention.**
  Product/e-commerce:
- **Return rate, contribution margin per SKU, inventory turns.**
  Subscription/SaaS:
- **MRR/ARR growth, churn %, LTV:CAC, gross margin.**

Pick 5–7 KPIs max. Plot **3/6/12-month** trends, not just one month.

D. Do variance analysis (what moved and why)

- **Budget vs. Actual:** Highlight variances >10% or >$1,000 (choose a rule).
- Ask: **Volume? Price? Mix? Timing? One-off?**
- Document a one-sentence **root cause** and a **countermeasure** for each big variance.

E. Segment the numbers (where the gold hides)

- **By product/service line:** Which lines carry your margin?
- **By channel:** Retail vs. wholesale vs. online—different margin and returns.
- **By customer cohort:** First-time vs. repeat; which cohorts are most profitable?
- **By location/project/manager:** Use **classes/tags** in your software to enable this.

F. Hygiene checks (avoid report distortions)

- No large **uncategorized** or **ask-my-accountant** buckets.
- **Prepaids/deferrals** posted (insurance, subscriptions).
- **Inventory** adjusted for shrink/spoilage at month-end if applicable.
- **Debt schedules** match lender statements.
- **Owner draws/distributions** booked correctly (not as expenses).

Practical examples (how this changes decisions)
Example 1 — Gross margin slide:
P&L shows revenue up 8% but gross margin % fell from 52% → 44%. Balance Sheet shows inventory jumped.

- **Action:** Audit COGS (supplier increases? discounts?), cull slow SKUs, adjust pricing, negotiate terms.

Example 2 — Profitable but cash-poor:

Net income positive, but **operating cash flow negative**. A/R Aging shows 38% in 60+ day bucket.

- **Action:** Tighten terms to Net-15 for chronic slow payers, enable ACH/card payments, auto-reminders, offer 2/10 net 30.

Example 3 — Hidden winner:

Segmented P&L shows one service line at **68% contribution margin** with low churn.

- **Action:** Reallocate ad spend, build upsell bundles, train sales to lead with that offer.

The mantra

Don't ask, "What are the numbers?" Ask, "What are the numbers telling me to do?"

When you review reports monthly, trends surface early, cash stops being a surprise, and strategy becomes evidence-based— not gut-based.

Waiting Until Tax Season to Get Organized

The Mistake:

- Scrambling every March/April to pull together receipts, invoices, and statements.
- Treating tax filing as a one-time event instead of part of ongoing business management.
- Assuming your accountant will "figure it out" at the last minute.

Why It Hurts:

- You **overpay taxes** because deductions and credits slip through the cracks when records aren't maintained throughout the year.
- Your **stress skyrockets** as you spend nights and weekends sorting through piles of paper and emails.
- Accountants and CPAs **charge more for clean-up** work — and they'll have less time to strategize on saving you money.
- Last-minute chaos makes it impossible to step back and see the bigger picture of how your business is really performing.

The Fix:

- **Treat accounting as ongoing, not seasonal.** Good businesses treat bookkeeping like brushing teeth — something you do regularly to prevent costly problems later.
- **Block time monthly (or weekly).** Put a recurring appointment on your calendar to update your books, review transactions, and reconcile accounts. Even one hour a week can keep you ahead.
- **Leverage technology.** Cloud-based software can automatically import bank feeds, categorize expenses, and generate tax-ready reports.
- **Go paperless.** Use apps to snap photos of receipts the moment you get them — no shoebox required.
- **Partner with an Accounting Firm.** If you can't realistically stay on top of it, outsource. An accounting firm can keep everything current, so your accountant focuses on tax strategy instead of cleanup.

- **Think beyond April 15.** Year-round bookkeeping helps
  you make smarter decisions, secure financing faster, and
  avoid surprises when tax season comes.

Bottom Line

Small business accounting mistakes are not just clerical errors —
they're **profit leaks.** Every missed deduction, misclassified
worker, or unpaid invoice chips away at your hard work.
The difference between thriving and struggling often comes
down to discipline in the boring stuff: separating accounts,
reconciling monthly, reviewing reports, and keeping receipts.

The entrepreneurs who win aren't necessarily the smartest —
they're the ones who **treat accounting like the backbone of
their business, not an afterthought.**

Chapter 9 – Managing Business Debt Without Losing Sleep

Debt is one of the most emotional parts of running a business. It can feel like a heavy backpack you can't take off — weighing down every decision, every night's sleep, and every dream for growth.

But here's the truth: **debt itself isn't the problem**. Debt is neutral. What matters is how you manage it.

Used wisely, debt becomes a tool — a lever that helps you buy equipment, hire staff, or bridge cash flow gaps. Left unmanaged, it becomes a trap that siphons profits and energy.

The Constructive Side of Debt

When managed properly, debt can:

- **Accelerate Growth** — Funding a second location, expanding product lines, or entering new markets without waiting years to save up the capital.
- **Smooth Cash Flow** — Bridging the gap between when you pay suppliers and when your customers pay you.
- **Unlock Opportunities** — Acting quickly on a time-sensitive purchase of discounted equipment or bulk inventory.
- **Build Credit History** — Strengthening your business credit profile for future, larger financing.

This kind of debt is an **enabler** — it helps you move faster, operate more smoothly, and take advantage of opportunities that might otherwise slip away.

The Destructive Side of Debt

The flip side is when debt is:

- **Unmanaged** — No clear plan for repayment or even a full awareness of how much you owe.
- **Unmonitored** — Interest rates and terms left unchecked, even as they creep upward.
- **Misunderstood** — Borrowing without understanding the cost, impact on cash flow, or risk to assets.

This is where debt stops being a tool and starts being a weight — draining resources, causing stress, and boxing you into fewer and fewer options over time.

This chapter will show you how to take control of your business debt, step by step, so it works for you instead of against you.

The Mindset Shift: Debt as a Tool, Not a Monster

Many entrepreneurs fall into one of two traps:

1. **The Avoider**: "If I don't look at it, it can't hurt me." They ignore balances, let interests pile up, and only act when creditors start calling
2. **The Overpayer**: "Debt is bad — it all has to go!" They throw every available dollar at loans and credit

cards, leaving nothing for marketing, hiring, or growth.

Both approaches cause problems. The avoider's debt snowballs. The overpayer ends up strangling their own growth.

Instead, shift your mindset:

- Think of debt as **fuel**. Gasoline can make your car go farther — but only if you use it properly.
- Debt is **leverage**. Borrowed money lets you do today what you might not afford until years later.

The key is **balance**. Not too much, not too little — just enough to help your business grow without controlling your life.

Step 1: Know Exactly What You Owe

Anxiety around debt is often a symptom of **uncertainty**. When everything is scattered across different accounts, credit cards, and loan portals, you end up with a vague sense of "I owe too much" instead of a clear plan.

Action Step: Create a Debt Snapshot

Build a simple one-page document (Excel, Google Sheets, or even a notebook) that lists:

- Lender/creditor name
- Type of debt (credit card, term loan, line of credit, equipment lease, etc.)
- Balance owed.
- Interest rate (APR)

- Minimum payment
- Payment due date
- Loan maturity date (if applicable)

Why this matters:

When everything is in one place, the monster under the bed turns into a list of action items. Suddenly, the unknown becomes known.

Example: A café owner listed out her debts and realized that one $5,000 credit card with 23% interest was costing her more each month than her $20,000 equipment loan. Just seeing that on paper made her priorities obvious.

Step 2: Understand the Cost of Debt

Not all debt is equal. Some are dangerous, some are neutral, and some are downright helpful.

- **Toxic Debt:** High-interest credit cards, merchant cash advances, payday-style loans. These bleed cash flow and should be eliminated ASAP.
- **Neutral Debt:** Lines of credit and short-term working capital loans. They're useful for smoothing seasonal ups and downs but shouldn't become permanent crutches.
- **Growth Debt:** SBA loans, equipment financing, or other low-interest loans tied to assets. If the ROI on the borrowed money is higher than the interest rate, this is "good debt."

Quick Rule of Thumb: Ask yourself: *"What return am I getting on this borrowed dollar?"* If the borrowed money helps you make more than it costs, it's a good trade. If not, it's dead weight.

Step 3: Choose a Paydown Strategy

Once you've organized and ranked your debts, you need a plan to pay them down. Two proven strategies dominate:

1. **Debt Avalanche (Math-First):**
   o Pay minimums on everything.
   o Throw extra money at the highest interest rate.
   o Saves the most money long term.
2. **Debt Snowball (Momentum-First):**
   o Pay minimums on everything.
   o Throw extra money at the smallest balance.
   o Builds psychological wins, which keep you motivated.

Which should you use?
- If you're disciplined and love efficiency → Avalanche.
- If you're motivated by quick progress → Snowball.

Case Example:
A consulting firm had three debts:
- $7,000 credit card at 19%
- $18,000 SBA loan at 5%
- $12,000 equipment lease at 9%

They used the Avalanche method, targeting the credit card first. By focusing on extra payments there, they saved over $2,800 in interest over three years.

Step 4: Automate and Systematize Payments

One of the easiest ways to lose sleep is to miss a payment by accident. It creates late fees, hurts your credit, and keeps you on edge.

The Fix:
- **Automate minimums.** Every debt should be on auto-pay for at least the minimum due.
- **Schedule extra payments.** Don't rely on memory — set a recurring calendar reminder to send additional payments.
- **Apply windfalls.** Got a tax refund? A surprise client payment? Allocate a portion straight to debt reduction before it disappears into operating expenses.

Step 5: Restructure If Needed

If your debt load feels overwhelming, you might not need to work harder — you might need to restructure smarter.

Sometimes, the most effective way to make progress on debt isn't just throwing more money at it — it's changing the debt itself.

By restructuring, you can lower your monthly payments, reduce your interest costs, and simplify your repayment plan. But this move requires careful consideration to ensure it sets you forward rather than traps you in a new cycle.

When people think about paying off debt, they usually imagine making bigger payments or sending extra money toward the balance each month. While that's effective, it's not the only lever you can pull. You can also *change the structure* of the debt so that:

- The **interest rate drops** (meaning less of your payment goes to interest and more goes toward principal).
- The **terms improve** (so your repayment plan is more predictable or affordable).
- The **number of payments you juggle is reduced** (making it easier to stay organized and avoid missed deadlines).

If you're carrying debt at high interest rates — say 18% on a credit card or 12% on an equipment loan — a refinance or consolidation can instantly reduce how much you owe in interest over time.

Options include:

- **Refinance:** Replace high-interest debt with lower-interest loans.
- **Consolidate:** Combine multiple payments into one. Often lowers your average rate.
- **Negotiate:** Lenders sometimes reduce rates or extend terms if you've been consistent but are showing signs of strain.

Example: One small manufacturer had three business credit cards totaling $40,000 at 20% interest. By consolidating into an SBA-backed loan at 7%, they cut their monthly payments by $600 and freed up cash for payroll.

The Catch — Why This Can Backfire

Restructuring isn't free money. You have to watch out for:

- **Longer terms** that reduce your monthly payment but extend the life of the loan, increasing total interest paid.
- **Closing costs or fees** that eat into your savings.
- **Temptation to re-use the old credit lines** you just paid off, which puts you right back where you started.

Done strategically, restructuring buys you breathing room in your budget and frees up cash flow for reinvestment or faster debt payoff. Done carelessly, it can quietly increase the total you pay and prolong the debt burden. The key is to calculate the real cost over the life of the loan *before* making the move

Debt Restructuring Decision Checklist

- **Interest Rate Test**
    - New rate is lower than the current blended interest rate.
    - Savings in interest are significant enough to justify any fees or costs.
    - Avoid if the "lower" rate is only a short-term teaser that will rise later.
- **Total Cost Over Time**
    - Compare the total interest you'll pay under the new loan vs. the current set-up — not just the monthly payment.
    - Don't be fooled by a lower monthly payment if the total paid over the life of the loan is higher.

- **Term Length**
  - Keep the repayment term equal to or shorter than your current remaining term (unless you *intentionally* need cash flow relief).
  - Avoid unnecessarily stretching payments over many extra years unless survival cash flow is at stake.
- **Fees & Penalties**
  - Know all upfront costs — origination fees, balance transfer fees, prepayment penalties on old loans.
  - Avoid deals where fees eat up a big chunk of your interest savings.
- **Cash Flow Impact**
  - New structure should free up cash for either faster payoff or reinvestment in the business.
  - Avoid using freed-up cash as an excuse to increase non-essential spending.
- **Behavior Check**
  - Commit to not running up new debt on the old accounts you've paid off.
  - If you've struggled with discipline in the past, consider closing or lowering limits on the old lines.
- **Exit Strategy**
  - Have a clear plan for when and how you will finish paying off the restructured debt.
  - Avoid "just seeing how it goes" — lack of a plan often leads back to square one.

Refinancing: Swapping Old Debt for Better Terms

Refinancing means replacing an existing debt with a new one — ideally with better terms that work in your favor. Instead of simply working harder to pay off a costly loan, you change the loan itself so it's cheaper or easier to manage. The new loan pays off the old one in full, leaving you with only the new repayment schedule to follow.

Refinancing can benefit your business in several scenarios:

- Interest rates have dropped since you borrowed – If market rates are significantly lower now than when you first took out the loan, refinancing can reduce the amount you pay in interest over the life of the loan. Even a 1–2% drop can mean thousands in savings on large balances.

- Your business credit profile has improved – Over time, paying bills on time, lowering existing debt levels, and building a longer track record can improve your business credit score. Lenders may then offer you lower rates or better repayment terms than you could access before.

- Switching from variable to fixed rate – A variable interest rate may start low but can rise unpredictably, making budgeting harder. Refinancing into a fixed-rate loan locks in your cost of borrowing, providing stability and making cash-flow forecasting more accurate.

- Lengthening the repayment term for breathing room – Extending the term lowers your monthly payments, which can free up cash for operations. This can be a temporary relief strategy if your business is in a seasonal downturn. However, keep in mind this usually means paying more interest over the life of the loan.

- Consolidating multiple debts into one payment –
  Refinancing can also be part of a broader debt
  consolidation strategy, merging several higher-cost loans
  or credit lines into one loan at a lower blended rate,
  simplifying your bookkeeping and payment schedule.

Caution: Refinancing is not automatically a win. Extending your repayment term too far can cost you more in the long run. Also, watch for fees, prepayment penalties, or "teaser" rates that increase after a specific amount of time. Always calculate the total cost of the loan over its entire life — **not just the monthly payment** — before deciding.

Pro Tip: When refinancing, compare the total cost over the life of the loan — **not just the monthly payment**. Extending the term too much can lower your monthly bill but cost more in the long run.

Debt Consolidation Loan: One Payment, Lower Rate

Debt consolidation is the process of taking out a new loan to pay off several existing debts at once. Instead of juggling multiple balances with different due dates, interest rates, and payment amounts, you replace them with **one loan, one payment, and one interest rate**.

The goal is to simplify your repayment plan, save on interest, and give yourself a clear end date for being debt-free.

Key Advantages

- **Lower Blended Interest Rate** – If your existing debts carry different rates (e.g., credit cards at 18%, equipment loan at 10%, line of credit at 12%), a consolidation loan can "blend" them into a single, lower rate — often saving you significant interest over time.
- **Single Monthly Due Date** – No more tracking five different payments across the month. With consolidation, you have one due date, making cash flow management much easier and reducing the risk of missed or late payments.
- **Clear Payoff Timeline** – Credit cards and revolving credit lines can feel endless because the balance can be carried indefinitely. A consolidation loan has a fixed repayment schedule, giving you a defined finish line.

When It Works Well

- **You qualify for a substantially lower rate** than your current average interest rate.
- **You have several short-term debts** that can be rolled into a single medium-term loan without extending the total payoff time too much.
- **You're committed to not running up new debt** on the accounts you just paid off. Closing or limiting access to those old credit lines is often part of the strategy.

Potential Risks

- **Paying more interest overall** – If you extend your repayment term too much, your monthly payment might drop, but the total interest paid could rise.
- **Temptation to reuse paid-off credit** – Many people fall back into debt if they don't address the spending habits or cash flow issues that caused the debt in the first place.
- **Fees and Penalties** – Some loans carry origination fees or early repayment penalties on the debts you're consolidating. Always factor these into your cost comparison.

Benefits:

- Simplifies cash flow management — one payment instead of juggling several.
- May qualify for a lower rate by using collateral (e.g., business property or equipment).
- Creates a defined "end date" for the debt, unlike revolving credit lines.

When to Proceed — and When to Pass
Go for it if:

- The **new rate is meaningfully lower.**
- You've calculated the savings after factoring in fees (origination, closing costs, etc.).
- You have a clear plan to avoid taking on new debt in the accounts you just paid off.

Avoid if:
- The lender offers a lower monthly payment but stretches the loan so far that the total interest cost skyrockets.
- Fees erase the savings from the lower rate.
- You're tempted to reuse paid-off credit lines, which can lead to **double debt trouble.**

Smart Safeguards for Restructuring
1. **Freeze or close paid-off credit lines** unless you need them for emergencies.
2. **Run the numbers** with a loan calculator before committing — look at total interest paid, not just the monthly bill.
3. **Negotiate fees** — some lenders will waive or reduce them for strong applicants.
4. **Time it right** — refinancing is most effective when your credit score and business performance are at a peak.

Step 6: Separate Business and Personal Debt

One of the most damaging mistakes entrepreneurs make is mixing personal and business debt. Swiping your personal credit card for office supplies seems harmless — until tax time (or worse, bankruptcy).

Why separation matters:
- Keeps bookkeeping clean.
- Ensures deductions aren't missed.
- Protects your personal credit score from business swings.

Action Step:
- Open a dedicated business credit card.
- Route all business spending through it.
- Use accounting software to track and categorize automatically.

Step 7: Monitor, Don't Ignore

Debt management isn't a one-time fix — it's an ongoing habit.
- **Monthly:** Review balances, payments, and interest charges.
- **Quarterly:** Compare progress to your paydown strategy. Adjust if needed.
- **Annually:** Revisit whether refinancing or restructuring could save you money.

Pro Tip: Treat your debt review like a "financial checkup." Just like you wouldn't skip a doctor's visit, don't skip looking at the health of your debts.

Step 8: Balance Debt with Growth

Some owners fall into the trap of **paying off debt at all costs.** While admirable, this can backfire.

Imagine: You pay off every loan — but then a $100,000 growth opportunity comes along, and you can't take it because you have no capital.

Healthy businesses do three things at once:
1. Keep a cash cushion for emergencies.
2. Invest in growth (marketing, hiring, systems).

3. Pay down debt steadily.

Debt should shrink over time — but not at the expense of your future.

Step 9: Watch Out for Red Flags

Debt crosses into danger zone when:
- **You're paying debt with more debt.**
- Vendors or employees aren't paid on time.
- You avoid opening bills or statements.
- More than 30% of your revenue is eaten by debt service.

If you see these signs, act fast. The earlier you intervene, the easier it is to course-correct.

Step 10: Get Professional Help Early

You don't have to do this alone. A good accountant, bookkeeper, or financial advisor can:
- Build a personalized paydown plan.
- Spot refinancing opportunities.
- Help project cash flow so you avoid future crunches.

Free Resources:
- Local **Small Business Development Centers (SBDCs)**
- **SCORE mentors** (volunteer experts)
- Local chambers of commerce often host financial literacy workshops.

The Payoff: Sleeping at Night Again

Debt doesn't have to keep you awake. When you:

- See the full picture,
- Prioritize strategically,
- Automate payments, and
- Treat debt as a business tool —

— you shift from being controlled by debt to being in control of it.

And the result? Peace of mind. The ability to think about growth, not just survival. And, maybe best of all, the chance to finally get a good night's sleep.

Closing Chapter – Turning Knowledge Into Action

You've reached the end of this book, but really, you're standing at the **starting line** for a stronger, healthier business.

We've covered a lot together: how to make accounting a habit, avoid common financial mistakes, manage cash flow, read your reports like a pro, and handle debt without losing sleep. Each chapter gave you tools, examples, and fixes you can apply immediately.

But here's the truth: **knowledge isn't power until it's applied.**

Business owners often finish a book like this thinking, "I need to overhaul everything." That's a recipe for overwhelm — and for giving up.

Instead, pick on habit to start. Maybe it's reviewing your financials every Friday morning; pick one system to improve. Maybe it's moving from spreadsheets to accounting software; pick one conversation to have. Maybe it's finally asking your accountant to explain your cash flow.

Small steps compound. Like compound interest, they grow into something powerful over time.

Most entrepreneurs think of accounting as paperwork. A chore. A cost. But if you've read this far, you now know better: accounting is your **decision-making engine**. It tells you whether to hire, when to expand, which customers are profitable, and where your money is actually going.

When you treat accounting as a strategic tool instead of a tax-season burden, or simply as a monthly expense, you stop playing defense and start playing offense.

Your Business Is a Story — Let the Numbers Tell It

Every number in your books is part of your business's story. Sales show what the market values, expenses reveal your priorities, and your cash flow tells whether your story is sustainable.

If you ignore the story, you risk writing a bad ending. If you listen to it, you gain the power to shape the next chapters of your success.

Remember: the best businesses don't succeed because the owner does everything. They succeed because the owner builds the right **support system**:

- A bookkeeper who keeps things current.
- An accountant who translates data into strategy.
- Advisors, mentors, or peers who hold you accountable.

Asking for help isn't weakness — it's leadership.

Don't spend years in "survival mode," focused only on the next bill, the next payroll, the next tax return. The systems you've learned here are how you shift into **growth mode**. When you know your numbers, manage your debt, and keep your books current, you free up time and energy to actually run the business you dreamed of building.

One Final Thought
At the end of the day, business isn't about spreadsheets, taxes, or debt. It's about creating something of value — for your customers, your employees, and your own life.
Numbers are just the map. They show you where you are, where you've been, and where you can go next.

So, take what you've learned here, apply it one step at a time, and write the next chapter of your business with clarity and confidence. Because the real goal isn't just managing money. The real goal is building a business you're proud of — and sleeping soundly at night while you do it.

About the Author

Antonio Pascarella is the founder and principal of Pascarella Accounting Group, LLC, where he has worked with hundreds of small businesses, guiding owners to turn financial confusion into clarity. With years of hands-on experience in accounting and consulting, Antonio focuses on making numbers approachable and actionable so entrepreneurs can build confidence and achieve sustainable growth.

Through his work at Pascarella Accounting Group, LLC, Antonio has helped business owners simplify their financial systems, avoid costly mistakes, and use accounting as a tool for growth rather than a source of stress. His approach blends professional expertise with a deep understanding of the rea-world challenges small businesses face every day.

In addition to his financial expertise, Antonio has a strong background in technology. He develops web and software solutions that help streamline business processes and empower owners to spend less time buried in administration and more time focused on strategy.

When he's not guiding clients or building financial strategies, Antonio enjoys astrophotography, software development projects, and DIY builds — always bringing the same curiosity and problem-solving mindset to his hobbies as he does to his work with business owners: a desire to simplify, clarify, and make complex things understandable.

www.ingramcontent.com/pod-product-compliance
Lightning Source LLC
Chambersburg PA
CBHW071608210326
41597CB00019B/3452